The Wooden Tongue Speaks
Romanians: Contradictions and Realities
by Bogdan Tiganov

**SUBCULTURE.
BOOKS**

The Wooden Tongue Speaks-
Romanians: Contradictions and Realities
by Bogdan Tiganov
A Subculture Books Original

All Rights Reserved, including the right of reproduction in whole or
in part in ant form.

Copyright © 2008 Bogdan Tiganov

First Edition
Subculture Books, LLC 2008

ISBN: 978-0-9799194-3-5

Manufactured in the United States of America

*Dedicated to my parents, my grandparents, Don, Dana, Nichita Stănescu and,
of course, the people of Brăila*

Publisher's Note:
You will notice that the formatting in this book has been done in such a way to
provide the reader with Tiganov's writing line by line. We felt strongly after first
reading his manuscript that there are lines included in this collection that had
the power of poetry, and should therefore be presented as such. We invite you,
the reader, to consume this collection as a hybrid of poetry and prose.

Short Stories	Page
A Personal History of a City Called Brăila	7
River Cut In Two	20
The Fight	26
Lost and Found	33
A True Miracle	45
The Fourth Floor	53
The Children	59
It's Marlboro	76
In the Mind	84
Yogurt	92
A Father	94
The Old Man's Village	103
An Interview	112
The Killer	121
Jesus, Where Has Everything Gone?	134
The Heart of a Woman	143
The Meal	153
The Verdict	163
Gap	174
The Poet of a Thousand Love Poems	184
Goodnight Work	192
Cold	199
Green	206
End (Justice)	214
Poetry	219

A Personal History of a City Called Brăila

It bothers me to think that I was being listened to, that my phones were tapped, my walls too, and the neighbors had glasses up to theirs.
In fact the walls were so thin there was no need for glasses.
As a boy I could hear how my neighbors upstairs chased each other and the woman screamed:
"Help!"
But nobody stopped her husband.
I couldn't whisper a joke about Ceaușescu[1] without being told to "Shh."
I realized it even then.
I knew I couldn't say everything I wanted or everything that came to mouth, but that was fine.
I now know not everything that comes to mouth is useful.
Not everything, if anything, is worthwhile.
But there in my home, and in my grandparents' home, what was there to listen to?
Why would it interest anybody else?
Do you want to hear how my parents are unbelievably tired and bad-tempered, shouting at each other because they can't understand each other's point of view?
You don't want to hear that.
You can hear that in your own home.
I certainly didn't want to hear it.
Do you want to hear what we're screaming at our new color television?
We're screaming:
"Bullshit!"
because we no longer believe what you're showing us.
You're telling us how everything's rosy and how we're the best but I don't see that on the table.

---

[1] *Nicolae Ceaușescu (1918-1989) was the President of Romania from 1965 to 1989.*

My table's empty and I'm hungry.
The electricity's gone off.
We light some candles.
The walls start shaking and so does the floor.
Do you want to listen in to our panic as we hold on to what we have so it doesn't smash on the floor and we lose it all?
Nature tells us that we're fragile.
At times, during our exile, we wanted to leave the problems of living in a foreign country as refugees and go back home to what we thought we knew.
Would you swap isolation and loneliness for love?
The love, we felt, would not come simply from our family, but from the very trees and the earth that uprooted them.
The expressions on peoples' faces would make us feel like we belonged.
Be it poor, sad, heartbroken, happy, delirious.
We had these fantasies.
I know I still get flashes of fantastic euphoria though I know that they're as much bullshit as what the Communists were feeding us.
I've learnt to mistrust the easy answer.

Maybe you're so interested in my family because television's not enough for you, your life is not enough, so you start listening and reporting, ratting and spreading lies about us because you are now a fully-grown unshakable demon of a pervert.
You're addicted to what we're having for dinner, hooked on to our morning routine, how mama brushes my hair or how tata[2] shaves, how many plops you hear in the toilet.
You're in love with our dreams and imagination, how innocent, naïve and terrifying.
Most of all, it bothers me to think that some element of happiness or sadness or honesty was lost because we were hiding it from you.
We didn't want you to know how deeply scarred we were, our stomachs slashed inside and our hearts burning slowly on a spit, but all you heard was some hysterical laughter or howled cries.
That's all you heard.
What we couldn't hide.

---

2   *The Romanian equivalent of Dad.*

Bogdan Tiganov

And mama realized we're alive right now so why waste it?
Why give so much and receive so little?
What does it matter now though?
You must feel utterly satisfied sitting in your villa in the mountains with the eagles singing to you and a great big pitchfork impaled up through your anus and out of your mouth.
Enjoy the horrifying silence you created and upheld.

When people ask me where I'm from originally I say Romania.
If they know a bit more they will ask me another question.
What town or city?
I, in return, gulp to the anti-climax for nobody has ever recognized the city in which I was born.
In all the years of living in the UK, or Canada, not one person has said "Oh yes! I know Brăila!"
My city
(and I prefer the word city to the word town because town implies small and insignificant)
is nowhere, lost, hidden, dead.
Completely unknown.
No tourist would want to go there because no tourist guide has more than a paragraph devoted to it and what, after all, is a tourist without his tourist guide?
The way I look at it, my parents lived in Brăila for thirty-five years therefore it can't be that bad.
Geographically speaking, Brăila is situated in south-eastern Romania.
It's a hundred or so miles away from Bucharest, the capital, near Galați, in a zone called Muntenia although, ironically, considering the name, Brăila is flat.
I could say "Brăila is near Ukraine" or I could even say "Brăila is near Moldova" but it'd be received with a polite nod and a change of topic.
If you really want to know, Brăila is close to the Delta, a wetlands famous for its rare species of birds
(Bill Odie should go there)
and wild, untamed, vegetation.
I am proud of having been born close to wilderness in a city that nobody's heard of.

The Wooden Tongue Speaks

And you can't say that nobody lives there.
There are over two hundred thousand people living in Brăila, and over three hundred thousand in the county of Brăila.
And it's a multi-national, multi-cultural place too.
Jews lived there
(my grandmother's boss was Jewish and so was the great Mihail Sebastian),
Gypsies, Greeks and Russians, or Lipoveni as they are known locally
(like tata and his family).
It is true, though, I never once saw an African, Oriental or Asian person.
Not even on TV.
Or perhaps I'm lying.
I'm sure I saw Ceaușescu's best friend, Arafat.
My grandparents lived in a studio flat in an area of the city called Hipodrom.
What I remember was how magical their block seemed.
Surrounded by greenery, gardens, trees, flowers, and close to a playground.
There were kittens and puppies in the garden, under the stairs, trying to find a safe spot.
These were the vagabonds and we were friends.
I knew them all.
The one under the stair, the black cat and her litter in the garage, the dogs near the swings, the cat near the window and the bats in the night in the hole above the door.
Nature and my grandparents were linked and tied up to my levels of expectancy.
The architecture is and was basic and thin.
But it's calming and peaceful in its feeling of reassurance.

As the Americanized say, "It's ok."
The dogs are barking and I can't sleep.
"It's ok."
The neighbors beat their rugs in the back near where the cars are parked on uneven ground.
There is a hospital across the street on the right-hand side.
Again, it's rather gray, or a graying cream and gray seemed to neutralize our personal revolutions.

Bogdan Tiganov

Maybe we all said: "It's ok."
The hospital is an imposing block.
And next to the hospital there lies the sports center.
Here you can play table tennis, lift weights, go swimming or even grind it out on the clay courts.
The sports center is actually the start of the park which, I like to think, is an extension of my grandparents' garden.
I tried to help tataia[3], holding an old rake and digging in.
The speckles of earth cascaded over me.
He would say that we're letting the Earth breathe.
Then we picked the ripe tomatoes so that mamaia[4], who I could see at the window and who's forever in the kitchen, could use them in her stews.
Then we watered the rest.
We said hello to our peculiar lonely neighbor who was also working on his patch.
From there I saw the park that we used to frequent.
Walking.
Cycling.
Playing.
Falling over.
Crying.
Laughing.
Begging for sweets and candy floss.
In wintertime tobogganing down the snow and ice while being wrapped in layer upon layer of suffocating clothing.

When the circus came, tataia bought me a harmonica
(I still haven't learnt to play it).
I watched tataia cycle and move and I never pitied him.
I never thought 'Poor him, he's disabled...' and if I did think it I tried to block it out.
Tataia can do with one hand everything that any other man can with two working hands.
Not only that, but tataia can invent, put together a complex circuit and give reality an edge.

---

3   *My personal Romanian version of Granddad.*
4   *Romanian version of Grandma.*

The Wooden Tongue Speaks

"Don't do that!"
"Why not?"
"You're hurting that tree. It's weeping."
I tried to listen to the tree, bringing myself closer so that I could hear its terrible sobs from the pain I had inflicted upon it.

The main boulevards in Brăila are very Parisian, wide, expansive, and you're hardly likely to bump into anyone else while walking along.
There is a sense of false grandeur as you keep expecting to see something truly wonderful but never do.
It's only when you reach the agricultural center and the mayor's apartment that you are faced with a decent enough fountain with stairs leading down to a plaza where they have concerts from time to time near the Danube.
I would call it pretty.
But I would also say it's forever associated with taking tataia out for a walk and how he wanted to keep going because he was damn well invincible.

As soon as you leave the drab concrete blocks of the center of town you get to the crumbly architecture of the old town.
There is plenty of character to these buildings and they stand like mini-revolutions in themselves, stray dogs hugging the pavement searching for shade.
Here also is the theatre built in classical style.
And there's a small tranquil park whereby you come across a blue clock that I find mysterious.
Why is there a blue clock in the middle of this anonymous little city?
The Maternity Hospital is where I was born.
It was in the afternoon and, I like to believe, it explains why I love napping any time from one o'clock to six o'clock.
I feel like I'm back in the womb and there can be no better feeling.
Surely that's what drug addicts or space explorers yearn for.
Apparently, I was one of the longest and noisiest babies born that day.
This doesn't really explain why they kept me away from mama for a whole day, the bastards.
But I cried all night and one nurse, who must've hated my piercing

Bogdan Tiganov

howls, ripped open my right ear with her nails.
She ripped me open.
A newborn slashed open, blood was on me and pain was with me hours after birth.
Welcome to the world she said!
But my God how happy they were to see me after the hospital incident.
My family had a taste for rebellion and I, with a torn ear, was one of them.
More than once have I had Strauss' tune in my head when near the Danube because it's not only blue but long, deep and sparkles like a devilish mirror in summer or when the sun slides across and the seagulls come to survey their snacks.
Tata said he swam across it when he was young.
Oh the things one does when one is young!
A time of extraordinary achievement and failure and such a pity that it all must end when we settle down to the ticking of the clock.
If you cross the Danube you will reach a small island where Russians/Lipoveni attempt to live.
They struggle, isolated and pecked by the limitations of circumstance.
You will see a people stuck in time, unable to escape, a people so used to their strife that if you offered them gold on a plate they'd probably throw it in your face.

If you cross the Danube, sunlight will blind you and you will have time to romanticize, if only in your mind.
On another small island, close-by, people go to sunbathe and relax away from the busy torment of city-life.
At one time, Brăila was a port town.
Ships flowed to and fro and on these ships travelers hid to find distant lands.
Travelers like Panait Istrati, who went away, came back and then went away like he couldn't decide where to go and what to do in his search for meaning in a harsh world.
Panait Istrati, the Maxim Gorky of the Balkans say some.
Because of the ships, lots of people here once made a living.
In factories people worked to make parts for the ships.
Commerce came and commerce left.

The Wooden Tongue Speaks

Now it's gone.
Disappeared.

I loved going on the trams with tataia.
He would be so concerned about me, especially if I didn't have a seat.
I'd ask him a million questions, the whys and what's and where's.
That's where my aunt lives.
That's where my cousin is.
There's the church we go to at Easter.
That's the moon and it's following me.
But I heard about the crash the other day.
I hope we don't crash but I see the crash in my mind and how we're all going to die.
The tram flops to one side and we drop one on top of another and crush each other's lungs.
It makes my heart palpitate.
And yet I am here and have no choice in the matter.
I am here and I dare not leave.
I can't leave.
I can't leave this here moment right now here.
The trams are old metal.
They creak, moan, disagree with their route.
That's why I'm thinking about crashing.

The shopping center has changed.
You can now buy Western goods.
Everything's for sale.
Incredibly expensive fur coats even.
People open shops in their own homes.
Come in and buy this keyboard I'm typing on – why not?
Most shops have a wide variety of goods but the shops themselves look identical.
You could probably buy your deodorant, jeans and Shakespeare within twenty square feet.

Under my city there are lots of tunnels, escape routes built in the days when Romania acted as a Christian fortress against Islamic invaders.

Bogdan Tiganov

The tunnels were also used in the World Wars.
I wonder what happens when unrepentant earthquakes hit the city and the pylons are dug deep into uncertain holed earth.
It could be thought of as a balancing game, a juggling act.
While we're holding the furniture the earth's holding the building and God's holding it all up.
And, more importantly, where do the tunnels lead?
Where can a citizen escape to?
Heaven or hell?

If you close your eyes and reopen them you will see that Brăila has a potential for beauty.
We have the therapeutic Lacu Sărat[5] close to home where you can splash stinking mud on yourself and then float on the water.
Last time I went it was still free, or near enough.
We have parks.
We have old impressive buildings.
We have the Danube.
In fact I see great beauty every time I go back.
There is everlasting beauty in the broken people, in their mini-dictator's complexes, in their harsh, brutal, fresh and finished attitudes.
There is beauty when I hear something I don't like.
Something provocative.
I'm too thin!
Stick thin.
I haven't grown.
I don't eat enough.
I look pathetic.
I know I am but I don't want anybody actually telling me that!
I've seen true beauty on the faces of children who are running through the streets with the happiness of not knowing.
Great beauty in the manner of celebration – we'll celebrate Christmas even if we can't pay the bills!
We'll smoke our cigarettes even if we can't afford to eat!
That's right.
We do what is necessary.

---

5   *Salted Lake.*

The Wooden Tongue Speaks

A strong defiance rooted in time.
I wonder about some of the people I know: how do they keep going?
How can they work months without getting paid?
How do they put up with the corruption and bribery?
How can they not explode when everything, everything is a chore?
It must be their fort like defiance.
Donkeys in human clothing.
Beautiful.
Endless years living with a fear that shut up the mute.
Tough skin.
Impenetrable.
If you take away the rubble, these people are the architecture and the scenery.
The landscape.
They are born with an ingrown taste for survival.

We lived near the train station so we were always close to going.
My grandparents lived four or five tram stops away while tata's parents were nearer to the train station than us.
I didn't see them much.
I'm not sure if they didn't like me or accept me but they certainly did not accept mama so I presume I was next down on their list.
Communist mass-construction buildings are a definite eyesore and my block seems particularly ugly.
Come in through the parting in-between the concrete.
Smell the piss.
You can come and see the graffiti on the walls:
"Fuck your mother!"
"Suck my dick!"
Old people are disgusted by this.
Young people spit and smoke cigarettes.
The grounds are dusty and there's no greenery.
We used to play football on these barren grounds
(now my friends prefer dreaming),
kicking a heavy ball until our feet hurt and shoes busted and our ears got twisted or our hair pulled.
The cars are parked anywhere: pavement, road or curb.

Bogdan Tiganov

One evening, at dusk, we got home after picking mama up from the hospital.
When we stepped out of the car, a ball flew in front of us and I saw mama holding her face, her spectacles knocked off.
Tata shouted to a youth in the distance "Come here you bastard!"
The youth started running.
Tata ran after him.
They disappeared.
We went home and waited.
We waited, my heart alive and panicking me.
I kept asking mama what tata was doing, imagining at the same time, the possibilities.
Maybe he caught him and gave him the beating he deserved.
Maybe the young one was stronger.
Maybe he stabbed tata.
Impossible.
Tata would never allow that to happen.
I kept waiting for the doorbell to ring and eventually I heard it and ran to open the door.
Tata did not look too happy.
"What happened? What happened? Did you catch him? Did you give him a good beating?"
He smiled.
"I chased him round the neighborhood," and I imagined tata panting like a dog looking left and right, circling the houses, peeking over fences, "but I lost him."
I must've looked disappointed because then he said "Don't worry, when I see him, and I'll recognize him, I'll hit him good."
In all honesty, I wanted him to dish out justice to everything and everyone that hurt us.

From home, it was incredibly easy for me to get to school.
I would turn right from our block of flats and keep going straight, past the church, pizza place and park
(where we used to buy doughnuts),
then turn left to the Bălcescu School of Music.
Reading about Nicolae Bălcescu I'm not sure what I think of the man.

The Wooden Tongue Speaks

A radical stance sounds good but dying young and ill doesn't.
I've also read that people don't know the origin of the name Brăila.
I believe it comes from Braille because locals say "Even the blind can find their way to Brăila."
If you follow the tram route onwards from my home and then turn left you will reach the area where tataia built his house.
There are no big ugly blocks here, only small houses full of character, petite, as they were once upon a time.
The roads are hazardous.
Crater-like holes sort out the locals from the tourists.
If you don't know where that hole is you're in trouble.
And yet, cars and carts weave their way through in an astonishingly skillful manner.
The roofs are pointed with chimneys like in storybooks.
Fairy tales.
Through that small gate there is a garden on either side of the path leading up to the main door.
The toilet is usually outside, in the garden, having the appearance of a shed with a hole in the floor.
A hairy mutt is waiting for you in his kennel.
He's been waiting a long time for a fool, barking at everyone he doesn't know and when he'll get old and blind he'll bark at anything that moves.
There are probably chickens near the back and maybe a pig or two if we're lucky, if not we'll have to tuck in next door.
As you walk along this road, and you admire the sentiment of blissful communal living, you might see a few old men playing dice.
They'll be sitting on chairs with a small table between them and on that table there will be the game board.
They don't want to be interrupted.
A drink, maybe, but whining townsfolk babble forget about it.
You may also see someone dragging a wheelbarrow
(pushing their TV, fridge, or enough onions to last the season)
or kids playing in the street.
God knows what they're playing at running around like that.
What do they think freedom grows on trees?
Before you go you might like to stop over at the cemetery.
Here, tataia is buried.

Bogdan Tiganov

Close to his family and home.
Family members come and sweep the graves.
They usher a prayer, wave incense, and memories are strong enough to stifle.
But they don't go under.

They straighten their backs and attempt to appear dignified as they start their walk back.

River Cut In Two

In the morning she'd get up at six.
Until she got used to the changes.
Then she would get up at ten.
Or eleven.
Unfortunately, she cried a lot.
Until she couldn't see very well.
She tried ringing them.
They were busy, at work, on holiday, in the park, at the cinema, with friends.
So she cried even more and then stopped crying and looked out the window and tried to remember what her purpose was but could find nothing.
In the evening he would ring.
Sometimes.

"Do you miss me?"

"Of course I do..."

"Do you really?"

Their conversations were part of another life.
They were like history books.
In the morning she'd get up at six and start cooking but she soon realized cooking for one meant you didn't have to eat.
She always had problems with money, especially in her head.
Poverty has a way of making you believe.
She had enough money, but it's the pension: so low, it's the food and

Bogdan Tiganov

drink: so expensive.
The telephone was a money hungry nuisance.
The TV too, only the TV was more entertaining.
There was always something to watch on the many many channels, mostly junk, if not all junk, but it can cheer you up, it can make you remember things that probably weren't there, it can give you hope.
She forced herself to learn from fantasy.
What does she do for relaxation?
She goes to the cemetery, where she is reacquainted with the old boys and girls.
They knew something these young idiots don't.
They knew how to wait and how to work.
Sure we all had our problems, but we handled them with dignity.
We didn't drug ourselves or turn to prostitution.
We also knew how to have fun at the right time.
Our time is past, you know?
And she would talk to tombstones and graves and pictures and names for a good hour, cleaning the graves and lighting the candles, ushering a personal prayer while incense in a can blew its memories in a circle.
There was beauty only in God and the church.
It was the suffering of Christ that made everyday suffering ok.
She knew there were lots of icons, but Christ on the cross, in the local church, was very impressive.
There was something new and emotional about it every day.
Look at his poor hands, smooth and artistic, in contrast with the hard sharp nails.
Stare at his writhing body, curved in reflection, against the brutal lines of the wooden cross.
His face, sideways, eyes closed, head slightly tilted upwards towards God, salvation, and all the beggar kids praying, the little ones with dirty faces and dirty fingernails chewing on a bit of bread.
There is true righteousness here and no one can take it away.
You can't deny corruption and rich priests but that's the state of the country, too much wrong to try and right.
No one can take the suffering of Christ away.
She would stand, pained by arthritis, almost blinded by cataracts, and she would listen to the sermons.

The Wooden Tongue Speaks

God will come again.
She'd pray that God take pity on the guilty: friends, family, murderers, criminals, politicians, for they know not what they do.
Save them, God, forgive them.
She'd forgiven them, and if she could forgive then God could too.
Easily.
Some of the interfering old grannies were there –
"Still alive eh?"

"Yes, still alive, going strong, feeling healthy for my age. But my kids…did you hear what happened?"

They had a lot to talk about, but she was fed up with it now.
She was really fed up with it all.
"I need to go…sorry but I bought cherries and left them boiling in the pot…I'm making conserves…"

They'd know she was lying but couldn't understand why.
Sometimes she'd say "I can't talk, not now or ever again."

She wanted to go home, the beauty was over, the day had begun and ended.
She planned what she would do, have soup at one o'clock, sleep for a few hours in the afternoon, get up and watch TV for a couple of hours, maybe start reading a book.
Maybe but probably not: the eyes aren't up to it, I can't concentrate, then clean, it's so dirty, dusty.
There's not much to do.
Nothing.

★

"That's really nice, Rita, really nice," and he went off to the next student who was waiting patiently for appreciation like a good dog.

"I like that, Gary, I like it. I like the colors. You have a pleasant sense of color," and Gary smiled because he had no idea what he was doing.

Bogdan Tiganov

Rita, though, was the sort of student you could rely on.
You knew that at six, every Tuesday evening, Rita would be there paying her £9.50 an hour.
She was a doddle to teach.
She'd never disagree with you.
And she had a dazzling old smile.

"Rita, I'd like to have a word with you after class."

"Ok, yeah, no problem."

She was truly eager to hear what Joe, her calm, kind and interested teacher, would have to say to her.
Was she not good enough?
Was she too slow?
Was she annoying the others?
Should she practice more outside class?
She couldn't wait.

"Sorry about the secrecy," he said, smiling like a guru.
"I wanted to tell you that we're holding an exhibition, on Sunday, for all the promising local artists, and I was wondering would you be interested in coming along? You could even bring some of your work for the show. We'll put it up for you. What do you think?"

He smiled some more, his eyes asking for approval.

"That's wonderful, Joe. That really is great news. I would be delighted to come along!"

When she got home, tired from public transport humidity and itching from excitement, she told her husband about it.
"Why don't you come?"

"Oh, I don't know…yeah…probably."

The Wooden Tongue Speaks

"Why don't you like art, John?"

"I just don't get it that's all. I like it but for me art is something you put on the wall and forget about-"

"You don't like art! You've never spent more than a minute looking at what I do and you spend all afternoon playing golf or watching golf or reading books on golf. Bloody golf!"

"Women are all the same. You don't know what sport means to a man."

"I know what it means. It's an excuse to relive childhood, to play with balls of varying size. You want to feel like a little boy again, John. That's what it means, but it's never going to happen."

He wanted to bare his teeth.
"Don't you get tired of moaning? I'm exhausted from your whining. And let me tell you I'm sick to death of hearing you talk about art and France and Mozart and yoga and whatever the hell else you do. Can't you see from my face that I'm not interested? I don't care about philosophy or spiritual attainment or music or forms, shapes and colors. Can't you see, can't you understand that I haven't given a shit for over twenty years?"

"You're a horrible, nasty man…I honestly don't know the person with whom I've spent so much of my life with…"

"The feeling's mutual, darling."

But they'd be fine and invincible by bedtime.
You learn all about compromise.
You say things you don't mean.
They had worked out that when you say things you think mean something you find that they actually mean nothing.
And when you know that you say sorry.
That's compromise.

Bogdan Tiganov

John had a strange habit of waking up at two or three in the morning.
He'd go and watch American golf tournaments.
It calmed him down and most mornings Rita found him asleep on the sofa.
She'd make breakfast and the smell of bacon would wake him up.
Two or three hours later he would have the decency to wash.
She would try to get out of the house as soon as she could.
Retirement brought on free time and free time brought on lots of things she wanted to do.
And because John didn't want to do anything she did them by herself.
This changed her mind, revitalized her, revived her.
She would learn as much as she could as best she could.
She was confident and proud and she had every right to be.
That's why you work, right?
Work takes away your imagination and your time and your enthusiasm to do anything else.
When you retire, take your life back.

The cleaner came once a week, usually every Thursday at noon.
She was from Zimbabwe and she kept her smile up well.
She also kept her tone high to ward off unpleasantness.
But really, she was disgusted with the houses she cleaned.
She was absolutely disgusted with the money these rich, arrogant, filthy pigs paid her.
She would tell her boys "You wouldn't believe how these people live, they're not happy, I can tell. They're lonely, with all that money, they don't know what to do with it, remember what I'm telling you: money don't bring you happiness."

The Fight

Nicu, I couldn't tell you because I was a coward, but in the fight, there was no better man to have.
You carved the two-faced with words, like when you told your sister to: "Get out of my house! You're waiting for me to die you bloodsucking little bitch do you think you can buy me off with oranges?"
Two seconds, her expression turned saintliness to disbelief – hurt – anger.
And, at work, the boss informed his whispering workers they'd have to join the party if they wanted their splendid new wages.
It seemed easy.
Move your hand and scribble your name under the party.
Comrade, start thinking about food, family and survival.
Nicu, you were desperate for as much money as you could possibly get and more.
You were building a house by yourself, working your spare time in producing brick, drawing your plans, redrawing, smoking forty a day, digging a big hole for refrigeration; Christ they arched back in shock when you stood up in front of two thousand people and said out loud "Double the money…you over there, in your suit: you can start carrying iron when it's fifty degrees…I'll sit and watch…and I won't sign…the Devil won't sign…" but your friends and enemies signed, right?
Nobody ever asked you to sign anything again so you worked for less and borrowed money to finish the house.
It was harder to borrow money.
Banks wouldn't lend you that kind of money.
You came to rely on your fellow man and woman, like Dan: a friend of the family, who lent you cash but acted like a prick about it.
After handing you the notes he slithered in a gut retching comment like

Bogdan Tiganov

"If I were building a house, I certainly wouldn't spend so much money on insulation."
You turned deaf temporarily.
The house was crucial to raising your family.
You tried very hard not to snap.

Thinking back, Nicu had lost his family home when he was nineteen.
The Communists came and forced it off his hands.
He was the only man left in that house after his father and brothers had died in an accident.
Nicu, though, earned enough to keep his mother and sisters breathing.
But the Communists bludgeoned our humanity for their idea of communal living.
They came with guns and papers and rules and relocated people to newly built flats.
The Communists took Nicu's house, land, chickens and pigs.
They took the horses, and he loved the horses, especially Cezar, the one with the white mark down the left side of his face.
He loved brushing Cezar at five in the morning while waiting for the cock to crow, a peaceful start to an otherwise
restless and relentless day.
He'd tell people that getting knocked out by a horse is something else; stories, oh timeless, eloquent stories that he told while smiling, laughing… whether his stories were true I don't know, but the listeners were captivated.
Nicu's mouth could utter poetry that would leave a smile absurdly pinching your lips.

He liked to fish, going with his friend Nelu at night in an old boat set adrift in the Danube.
They would sit there and take turns stretching.
It was wide-awake cold as they slapped mosquitoes off their arms and legs and watched fireflies making their way near the bank.
It was also wonderfully quiet, a state of calm in which you're not having to give or receive, push or pull.
Only the float would interrupt their sleepy state, and, mostly they ignored it, the fish would have their meal and leave.

The Wooden Tongue Speaks

The two friends shared cigarettes and usually a bottle of wine to warm their moods and bellies.
Back on land there was a lot to talk about, a midnight stroll home full of optimism and gaiety.
His mind was his journal and he could remember just about everything in vivid light: from his birth to the somber nights watching his father muscle the land.
To the hospital where they said it was a miracle that he was alive to the night when he met Iozefina.
He was forced to slow down sometimes, to take each image and realize how the image had affected him.
The accidents and incidents that change a world.
His friends had told him about her.
She was a good girl.
Her father had died, starved himself to feed his family.
She came from her father's first marriage but she got on well with the new brothers and sisters and she worked in a pharmacy, mixing.
Nicu was in love when he held her the first time, a small but lively girl.
He remembered having to sleep with her in a little room next to the bathroom, and his mother and sister would have to walk past.
Constant interruptions.
But, hellish consequences aside, he would feel that, at times, she understood him completely, that her movements complemented his.
And he would listen to all their complaints, their bitterness and hatred.
There was no end to their advice and criticism.
"That's friends and family for you. Drilling a hole back to where you came from."
I have never heard truth sound so equally vicious and comforting.
Now some men shine manliness from their fingertips, without a moment's doubt in their minds.
It is a ridiculous act, a power struggle, and few men survive it.
Some turn on themselves, others try to impress further, continuing their descent down a staircase of mistakes.
Dan was in the army, and he prided himself on his strength: physically, mentally and financially.
He was also an informer.
That's what earned him a superior lifestyle.

Bogdan Tiganov

Nicu didn't know Dan was an informer but he found out one evening when Iozefina told him there were rumors Dan was shooting people in the back for not complying.
He went to Dan's the following evening.
And, yes, he soon got to the point.
"Dan, it would be good of you if you could-"

"Yeah, I know, lend you some money but I can't do that, right now is not a good time. I need it to put food on the table. Honestly, I can't afford to throw it away…"

"But it's people like me you should be shooting…you should do your job properly…"

Most people blush.
Most people feel anxious.
He had something to brush off his soul, some unasked for dirt.
He couldn't quite form his words for Dan, the words that he was supposed to come up with were no longer human.
"What? What?"

"You're shooting people in the back? How can you possibly have the balls to give me advice? You?"

There was no rest.
No time between the machine gun words.
"You what?"

"Backstabber. Animal."

Finite.
By this time the women had backed off to the tiny kitchen where they whispered to each other, hoping the violence would end, oh dear God…

"Traitor? Traitor to what?" and before Nicu knew it, Dan had pulled out a gun and was pointing it at his head.
It looked natural.

The Wooden Tongue Speaks

Dan had prepared himself for a moment like this.
Many a time he'd thought it through.

"You're used to it. It's easy for you. Come on. Shoot."
He wanted to shout, to yell his words, but his fear kept the words quiet
and he thought he would die.
His soul was truly his again.

"Don't come here again, Nicu. You're an impossible specimen…" Dan
said, throwing his gun on the sofa, turning his back on the scene.

★

The house was his life.
It was his stand against the bastards.
As a boy, real responsibilities prevented him from attending school, but he
learned much more by reading what he wanted:
Tolstoy, Jack London, Caragiale[6].
Some of his books had to go.
Years later, he was to buy those books again because he loved them
very much.
They were more than yellowing paper and black ink.
Some of the writers could tell him astonishing truths and ideas that
nobody around him could.
It was, admittedly, a way of escaping to distant lands he knew he would
not get the chance of seeing.
One life can't be enough.
When he had a bit of cash leftover, which was once every couple of
months, he would go to guitar lessons at the local music school.
The notes, the professor's talks on music, the sounds of picking and the
singing, everything about it was magic.
The lessons always ended abruptly and too soon for him but as he
improved he would go home, play guitar and sing to his baby daughter.
She would clap her beautiful tiny hands.
He also took part in local dances, traditional folk dancing, the feeling of
movement while holding a girl's waist, their different scents, and the

---

6   *Ion Luca Caragiale (1852-1912) was a Romanian playwright, novelist and short story writer.*

music would carrying him off for a while.
His wife was jealous but there's fundamental importance in the intimacy between people, a kiss, a touch, oh Nicu it was easy to learn from you.
All I had to do was watch you.
When he was fifty-two years old, Nicu had a stroke.
He collapsed, at work, his face cracked on the floor.
A friend came thinking he was playing one of his practical jokes, or was drunk.
But he wasn't.
And his jokes would not click as well again and he could not fight as effortlessly again.
He couldn't live like he had done.
He tried though, he fought.
That's what life's for, he would say –
"You fight from the moment you're born till the moment God takes you, satisfied with your efforts, get up bloody and throw another punch."

He learned.
Relearned.
Everything was new and yet he felt old so all of a sudden.
New pains multiplied exponentially upon his legs, his arms, his stomach, he felt dizzy, sick, valiantly trying to hide his frailties as long as possible.
What happened was that he started reliving the past.
Nicu realized there were moments that had gone far beyond his reach and vanished.
No longer could you spend endless hours on the Danube waiting for fish.
No longer could you work, and I mean real work, and you were a workingman, at home most in the hustle of work, in the sweat and blood and its never-ending cycle.
The stroke took that away from you.
Surely, it's not right to take so much away.
Nicu still had his mouth, and it wasn't a good idea to get on the wrong side of it.
His own family thought he had turned into a crazy old man, but they

The Wooden Tongue Speaks

knew he'd been shooting them the truth all his life.
It was convenient for them to forget how when he was nineteen he'd cleaned and fixed shoes, traveling up and down the country cleaning and fixing, saving money to feed their sour mouths.
They would never know that he loved those moments on the train when he was his own man, eating bread and cheese, not paying for his fare and sleeping wherever the inspector wasn't.
Working those trains, so many rich men with their crisp moustaches saying "Ok, son, you can clean my shoes."
Then, in-between, he feasted on the country, the tastes and smells from north to south, the flat sunflower fields and the rocky peaks nearing the heavens.
The women, the clothes, the perfume, the odor, the love, hate and arguments, the accents and attitude, the evening sky, the sunrise…

He had more rituals as an ageing man than before.
One vital ritual was riding the tram then getting off in the old town where there's no pavement, only great holes in the roads in which unfortunate cars can fall.
Here, where the children were just as hungry and joyous and beautiful as they had been fifty years earlier, Nicu walked slowly and carefully, using his walking stick, to the house he'd built.
He stood a fair distance away and looked at it.

The new owners have made it look pink and modern.
They've changed the layout.
No more swing or pig pen.
I wonder about these owners, when they'll show their faces, skin and bone.
It's possible they won't ever come outside.
He saw it in his mind, everything being built, rebuilt, destroyed, built, rebuilt, destroyed.
I'm sure there must have been tears or sweat only he kept his head still and his eye looking.

Lost and Found

Understand me sir I'm not the type who goes out looking for trouble.
I do my job, come home, have a drink, eat something, watch TV and rest.
But it's not easy to do any of that when you're alone.
And I mean alone for a long time.
Wait, I'll get to it.
Listen to me.
So yes, alone.
It's not easy to cope when you're by yourself.
You wake up and there's no one there.
You end up thinking an argument is better than nothing.
Yeah, so then you go to work and you try hard to smile.
You switch on your computer and look at the screen for hours until you feel your eyes have lost control.
You click, draw lines, design, type, write, your eyes moving fast, your brain always on to the next thing.
You come home from work and it's the same story.
You and the walls.
You and yourself and there's only so long until you have to finally face yourself.
The house is too quiet.
Somebody's about to break in and kill you any moment.
When it's so quiet you start thinking and feeling crazy things.
You think somebody's tapping on the window so you pull back the curtains ready with a knife in hand.
You think you haven't turned the oven off so you check ten times before you go to bed.
You think you didn't close the windows.
You think you didn't lock the door.

The Wooden Tongue Speaks

And one day you're right.
You didn't lock the door although you distinctly remember putting the key
in the door.
But the quietness and the loneliness made you forget to turn the key.
It's not enough just to put the key in the door, do you get me?
The answer, I thought, was marriage.
It's not something to laugh about.
Look at me.
I'm forty-three.
Overweight.
I'm a product designer.
You know those little bottles you stick in your nose when you've got a
cold?
Romania would be the best place to marry.
I was born there.
My mother's still there.
I know the mentality.
The plane landed at two o'clock in the morning.
I was exhausted and excited.
It seemed like I was the only human being in that airport.
I went outside for a cigarette and looked at nothing.
I always get that feeling with airports don't you?
You go somewhere, you land, you get out, and it seems like you're in
concrete nothingness.
That's especially true of Otopeni Airport.
When you see the view you think nobody could possibly live there.
Now stop me if I'm boring you.
Right.
Right.
Details.
I'll tell you all I remember but I'm not one for details.

There was no taxi so I called mother.
She sent a neighbor to pick me up and he couldn't, couldn't shut up.
Two o'clock in the morning and he couldn't stop talking.
By the time the hour's drive was over I knew all about his family.
He hated them all.

Bogdan Tiganov

He wanted to shoot them in the head one by one.
Then she came to greet me.
Mother was sleepy and moody and kept complaining but trying her best to sound like she'd missed me.
I had a beer and went to bed.

I stayed in for three days, sleeping or looking out the window.
What I saw was an identical block across the street, gray and heartless.
They'd killed most of the strays and I missed them.
Their madness gave character to the place.
I placed an ad in Evenimentul Zilei[7].
It read something like:
"Young, attractive bachelor looking to marry beautiful girl, 20-30 years old."
I also put in that I spoke English.
I was English and therefore worth something to a woman.

The fifth day I received a phone-call.
She was interested in the ad and wanted to meet me and, God bless her, she liked the sound of my voice.
So I met her and she was ugly, loud, rude and desperate to find someone more desperate than she was.
It was difficult to get away from her.
I couldn't even remember her name.
It was embarrassing like:
"Come on baby I really like you, don't you think I'm pretty?"

"Well...yeah."

"You aren't sure?"

"I...am...I..."

"You think I'm pretty don't you?"

"No..."

---

[7] *Romanian newspaper with a large readership.*

The Wooden Tongue Speaks

"What?"

Out of embarrassment I didn't tell mother what had happened.
But I had to be positive.
The holiday was for a fortnight and at the end of it I would be alone again and that thought had me panting and sweating like a mass murderer.

The sixth day nothing happened.
I waited for the phone to ring.
I walked round the block.
It felt like I was back in England.
I was watching too much TV.
Politics and sex.
Everything was about political change, only reality seemed dead stagnant.
And sex was on most channels, girls practically naked and smiling at you, but you couldn't see this on the street where they were serious and gloomy like the sky was too low for them.
The TV pumped a sense of security into them, and me.
And football was the only sport.
You'd think they were Brazil but they'd never done anything and only ever really had one great player who made it: Hagi.
It was sad, though, the way they hammered nationalism and patriotism into people.
I could imagine coming home from a shitty job that doesn't even pay enough for the rent, living in gray concrete blocks with a super intrusive family around my neck.
I could imagine this then and it really was a nothing day.

The next day was a Sunday.
I went to church and tried my best to pray.
For a moment it seemed like I had never left.

On Monday I got another call.
She sounded a bit frightened on the phone so I was apprehensive.
Her name was Diana and she said she was twenty-two.

Bogdan Tiganov

I put on gray trousers and a white shirt.
On the metro I got lost, not because I'm stupid but because you have no idea where the trains are going.
Really.
I called her.
I told her I would be late.
She said "That's fine."
I got there sweating and angry and I wouldn't've minded if she was the devil's cow.
I was in that sort of mood.
I rang the entry system thing hanging loose.
She answered and her voice wasn't as frightened.
I thought ok I'm here.
I told her I would climb the stairs to her place.
It was on the fourth floor.
She opened the door and for a moment I lost my balance for she looked like she could roll you down the hill to insanity just by moving her hips, a little to the left, a little to the right.
You don't really get this kind of feeling in England.
It's just chat, shag, get up, follow up.
This was red.
This was golden.
This was a slight young woman and I was a sweaty bastard with little or nothing to say.
The words were jammed in my throat and I thought I'd better leave before I make an idiot out of myself and she calls her father or brother or lover to beat the shit out of me.
A lack of confidence?
I say it's more like fear of flesh.
But it wasn't like that.
She shook my hand calmly and kissed me on the cheeks.
She joked about the metro.
I laughed.
We walked down.
We turned corners.
We ended up at her favorite restaurant.
It wasn't glitzy.

The Wooden Tongue Speaks

It was empty.
We took off our coats.
There was the usual stuff on the menu.
I didn't want ciorbă[8] so I went with the tocăniţă de porc[9].
I wanted a bottle of wine.
She agreed.
We weren't talking much, a relief to my ears.
I missed her every time she went to the toilet.
I was thinking what is she doing in there?
Trying to open the window far enough to jump?
But she came back and the meal continued.

I said "So what are you doing at the moment?"

And she answered "I've finished medicine. I want to be a doctor."

This kind of talk bores me so I had to think of something like "I know a few doctors and they're the craziest people I know!"
And I remember she didn't laugh.
She nodded, pained.

She asked me what I was doing and I said "I'm a designer" and for a moment before I answered I couldn't remember who I was or what I did like I didn't exist.

The meal finished, I paid, we put on our coats and left.
We walked in silence.
I didn't feel there was much chemistry but I liked her.
I liked walking beside her and knew I hadn't impressed her.
I knew that it would be the last time I'd see her.
We got near the door and I thought this is the last possible moment for her to show me some damn affection.
She kissed me on the cheeks and said: "See you soon."

I left, thinking I'd paid the bill and she hadn't thanked me.

---

8   *Soup, usually sour.*
9   *Pork stew.*

Bogdan Tiganov

It was over so quickly, from the cradle to the grave.
Diana phoned me the following evening.
She asked me over and by that time I hated her with a hatred built up from too much frustration.
The way she'd manipulated me into feeling good…
I also hated the way I rushed to her place, the way I was dreaming.
I ran upstairs and when she opened the door I jumped on her.
She'd made me.
And when I jumped on her we fell on the floor, me on top.
I didn't care if she was dead as I grabbed her slender frame and my hands searched for what I wanted.
I'm not very good at this sort of thing but I pushed her and kept her down and felt for my flies.
I bullied her as I slammed it in.
She didn't scream.
She didn't laugh.
There was a smile on her face but I tried not to look at her smiling because the smile seemed wrong.
It didn't last very long.

When I looked at her she was already dressed.
She asked me, from the kitchen, if I would like a cup of coffee.
I managed to say yes.
Then I got up, tucked my shirt in, and walked to the kitchen where I sat at the small table and waited.
She smiled again that very same smile.
I was breathing hard.

That evening we lay in bed in silence and didn't do much.
In the morning she said something about applying for a Masters and how difficult it was, but I couldn't concentrate.
We walked out together and she kissed me on the lips and I walked her to the metro and we took different trains.
I went back home where mother had lots of questions for me.
I tried my best to hide things.

We met at five o'clock.

The Wooden Tongue Speaks

She looked tired and we went out to the same restaurant.
This time I had ciorbă.
She seemed to brighten up.
At her place she put on some relaxing jazz.
I don't like jazz, but it was appropriate.
She talked about her Masters.
I listened.
I told her that I would have to leave, hoping we'd get to talk of marriage.
She didn't say anything.
I felt disappointed.
I was wondering what I was doing there, whether I was some kind of experience to her.
That's all they talk about these kids.
Experience.
I wasn't in the mood for action so I went to bed with a headache and woke up with the same headache only worse.
She was playing with me.
This doctor.
She was analyzing me like a piece of meat.
I decided to break it off.
I knew her number and didn't answer when she rang.
I was going back to England alone.
But first I needed to get out.
So I got on the first train.
Slow journey.
The couple opposite me told me that I was on the fast train.
Cripples passed through selling plastic crosses, pens and lighters.
I bought one of the pens.
I didn't even test it.
Just wanted to feel better about myself.
I watched the landscape.
Didn't see much.

I kept thinking about Diana.
Maybe it was my turn to be a bastard, and that thought cheered me up.
The couple, about my age, kept trying to speak to me.
I said a few words and hoped they would forget it.

Bogdan Tiganov

They asked me what I thought about politics.
And football.
I lied.
I went to the toilet and looked in the mirror.
I saw the rail tracks through the hole in the toilet.
I stayed in the corridor and smoked.
I got off somewhere, a haunted place with too many flags.
Then I went outside and said to a taxi driver:
"Take me to a good hotel…no…a very good hotel."

He said there were a few very good hotels.
Which one did I want?
The one by the river or the one by the shops?
I said "River."

At the hotel I drank too much at the bar and had to be helped up to my room.
I woke up on the floor and decided to call her.
She asked me where I was.
I said I didn't know.
A dead town.
She told me to come back, that she didn't understand why I was behaving like a child.
I gave in, paid my hotel bill, which was a rip off, and walked back to the station.
It was a long way and I kept asking people for directions.
I got on the slow train.
It was the same kind of journey as before.
When we met I was red in the cheeks.
We sat at the kitchen table and she said "What do you want?"

"I don't know…" I said "I want to marry you."

"Fine," like that- fine.

"We have to do it tomorrow," I said.

The Wooden Tongue Speaks

"Ok," she said.

Then she called a couple of friends.
They were to be the witnesses.
We went together as early as possible.
There was no weather that day.
People looked lost and I felt tired.
The registry office was very modern.
Black wood.
Shiny.
A very serious looking gentleman asked us to repeat the lines.
Then we kissed.
There was no music and no clapping.
There was no laughing and no dancing and no cake.

When we got home I told her I would come back for her in a week.
I told her everything would be alright, that she could do a Masters in England.
I'd pay for it.
She could pick up the language no problem.
It was an easy language.
Doctors were in demand.
British doctors were clueless.
I even did a little pantomime typing on an invisible computer to show her just how fucking easy everything would be.
She smiled.
Obviously, I believed in ghosts far more than she did.
On the other hand, I'd been waiting to say something like that all my life.

"Mother, I'm married."

"What?!"

"Yesterday."

"My God…my sweet Jesus…my God! My God!"

Bogdan Tiganov

She said I should do everyone a favor and turn myself in to the local asylum.

At the airport, where I get nervous, Diana kissed me.
She told me she couldn't wait to see me again.
She would be ready.
I got drunk on the plane.
I was in a haze at work.
I got told off by my boss.
I couldn't sleep.
I phoned her.
She wasn't answering…and a week later I was back in Otopeni airport.
It was around two o'clock in the morning and mother's neighbor picked me up again.
This time I liked his jokes.
Mother embraced me and told me she knew this would happen.

She said: "There are many opportunist whores here, son. Didn't you realize that? At your age?"

I didn't answer.
Who was the real whore here?

I had a couple of beers but I couldn't sleep.
I heard a stray dog barking.
Then I searched for her.
I rented a car and went everywhere.
Even asked her friends.
They didn't know.
They hadn't seen her either.
One of the girls – she had red hair and one of her eyes looked sideways – gave me your number.
You're the best she said.

It doesn't matter about the cost.
What I want is simple.

The Wooden Tongue Speaks

I want to know where she is.
I want an explanation.
Because I need her.

A True Miracle

"I swear to you this time I'm going."

"You say that every year."

"I do. A man's got to have a dream right? But this time I don't care what happens. I'm going."

I've been hearing this for too long but I've got to keep calm and not tell him to forget the whole leaving thing and concentrate on living here.
I want to tell him that people want to go somewhere else because they're weak, lazy bastards.
I look at him.
He's handsome and he's good at IT.
He's got a girlfriend and his apartment's fine.
He's even got a car.
And every year he's going to America.
He knows somebody there: a cousin, a friend, an uncle, an old girlfriend, there's always somebody he knows who will help him get there.
All he needs is a green card, but that's not a problem.
Nor is the money they require you to have in the bank.
There is no problem.
All the young people are leaving he would say, so why shouldn't I?
And it's worth it, by God it's worth it.
You get there with a contract and they give you a good job, maybe thirty thousand dollars a year.
And it's not like here.
If you do a reasonable job you get paid.
And you get paid well.

The Wooden Tongue Speaks

Thirty thousand dollars a year at least.
You get promoted.
You stay a couple of years, save up, come back home and live better than the president.
You get yourself a luxury mansion near Cluj.
You get yourself a black Mercedes.
And you won't have a problem supporting your family.
Don't you think that's worth it?

"Alright I'm off."

He looks hurt.
"Do you think I'm lying? Are you thinking that?"

"Yes."

He's getting emotional.
"You'll see. One day I won't be here. You'll ring my doorbell and they'll say: 'He left, yesterday.' You'll know the truth."

"Ok." I've heard enough.

I need to go somewhere and do something and relax.
I usually go to relax by swimming across the Danube and then by finding a place near the beach where nobody else goes.
I sit or lie.
I stare at the water or at the sky or at the sand.
I find it relaxing because the town is on the other side.
The water is between the town and me.
It's like cutting it off from my mind.
Too much: too busy, too many people wandering, too many dogs, too many liars, too many dreamers.
I miss the old ship.
It went bust.
No more old ship, slow trips, tranquility.
The Danube is bare.
Business is dead.

Bogdan Tiganov

There is no money and no jobs.
I understand the situation.
I'm probably the only one who wants to stay.
I was born here.
Some days, though, I want to swim downstream.
Today I want to explore.
I want to see.
This island was built for vegetation but it gets flooded easily.
Nobody could possibly live here.
You can see where the water comes to by looking at the tree trunks.
There have been a few deaths, stupid kids who didn't realize what was happening.
I get there early and instead of just lying near the beach I walk straight into the woodland.
It's cooler and I appreciate it.
Still, the sun finds its way through.
There are segments of sunshine, different shades of bark.
We forget all of this when we leave.

I see a wide slab of metal.
One hell of a discovery: a piece of metal so wide, several houses wide, in the middle of the woodland.
It's probably from the old ship.
What happened to the old ship?
Was it diced up and sold for scrap?
Or did it disintegrate naturally?
As I get closer I'm amazed by the size of the metal.
It is wider than I thought.
It is also very thick and strong.
And there is a clearing through the trees where the metal keeps going.
I can't see the end of it but it's possible to walk on it.
This discovery may not be incredible for someone else, who'd just shrug it off as a giant piece of metal, but it is incredible for me.
I didn't expect to find anything like this.
So I go on because there could be something even more incredible at the end.
It certainly feels stable enough under my feet.

The Wooden Tongue Speaks

I doubt even a bomb could destroy it.
The clearing expands and the sun makes everything too white
for my liking.
The sun reflects off the metal and I don't have my sunglasses.
I take off my t-shirt and carry it over my left arm.
It is forty degrees and humid.
And quiet, although I have loud sounds of trams blaring and car horns
repeatedly drumming in my mind.
I want my mind to be as quiet as where I am.
I want to be alone completely.
I keep going.
It seems like half an hour has passed, but I'm not sure without my watch.
Left my mobile home.
No messages or calls today.
It's the weekend and I don't want to work or study again.
The metal will probably lead me to the end of the island and back to the
Danube.
It's crazy.
It will take a long time to come back.

"Good morning."

I turn round.
I look around.
Did somebody speak?

"Hello?"

I feel like an idiot.
There's no response.
My legs have stopped.
I look around again.
Maybe other people have found this metal.
Maybe it's become a secret playground, a club for gangsters.

"Good morning," and I turn round, a giant of a man behind me, with a
strong blonde beard and sharp green eyes.

Bogdan Tiganov

His beard is over my head.
He looks down at me.
I try not to look like this could be the biggest shock of my life.

"Good morning."
It was the only thing I could manage.
It's pathetic the way we react, isn't it?

"Sorry to disturb you like that. I was inspecting the bridge, going over the details, and I saw you walking and I thought I'd come and say
good morning."
His voice is strong.
You could say, in your Hollywood voice, he is twice the man I am.

"That's alright. Don't worry about it. A bridge you say?"

"Yes, a bridge."
Why would there be a bridge on the island?

"Well, it's not quite a bridge yet. It will be soon. Very soon. And there's a lot more coming too. A lot more. You wouldn't believe me if I told you."
I really don't know how to respond.
"Not many people know about this bridge. It's not a secret, but not many people come so far. When it's finished we're going to raise it over the water."

"Why? Why do we need a bridge linking the island to the town?"

"It's a miracle."

"A miracle? Like Jesus curing the blind?"

"Yes! Absolutely!" he says and he smiles.

I can't see his lips, only his beard twitching upwards.
"Please tell me more."

The Wooden Tongue Speaks

"Can't. Signed a piece of paper so I can't."

"Ok. Where do I end up if I keep walking?"

"I'm afraid you'd better turn back now."

"Why?"
"You can't go any further. You're not allowed."

"Why? There are no signs here."

"You've got to wait like everybody else."

"What am I waiting for?"

"You'll see."

This talk is going nowhere so I decide to step back around him because if he says I can't go further then I believe him.
Don't argue with a giant.
The important thing is not to look like a loser.
Walk.

"Come back!"
I look.
I see him now, but he's not so big.
He's not really a giant.
He's a man like me.

"I can show you something."
I go to him.
He takes a crumpled piece of paper out of his jacket and gives it to me.
I smooth it out, or try to.
There's a picture of what looks like a ball.
Inside the ball there are stairs.
The stairs connect the levels.

Bogdan Tiganov

The levels have little squares.
There are little squares everywhere in the ball.
Around the ball there is the river.
The river has a bridge across it.

"I don't understand why we need the bridge."

"The bridge will connect the Power Station to the world."

"The world?"

"A world inside a world."

"Sounds good."

"An organic world. The Power Station too. No more deadly emissions. We're digging right in. We're taking power from north, south, east and west."

"Wow."

"That's not glass surrounding the world."
I look at the ball.

"That's our energy."
I look at the ball as if it's about to burst into life.
This is ridiculous.
It's a science-fiction dream in the middle of a reality that is too real, too painful and too cruel.

"Take the picture. Keep it with you. When you feel down, look at it. Think about it. This will change everything. And we're working on it non-stop. We're dedicated," and again he smiles.

"Thanks."

"Now go, and don't come back. Don't bring anyone back. There are

The Wooden Tongue Speaks

guards and they will arrest you. You don't want to be arrested. Here."
He offers me his hand.
I shake it.
It's the strongest, biggest hand I've ever shaken.
It's reassuring.
Then I take the piece of paper with the drawing of the ball on it, crumple it like it was originally, and stick it in my shorts.

I lie here and look at the water.
This water has seen it at all, the wars, the struggle.
This water is blue.
I can smell dead fish.
I think about the world.
I think about the bridge and the giant.
I think about the final handshake, how it made me feel.
I wish it were true.
I wish something like that happened.
I wish it would prove most people wrong.
I wish I'd be there to see it.
I want to see their expressions change.
I want to see someone smile.
I want to see everybody smile and lift their heads up.

I think about how glorious that will be.

The Fourth Floor

The football got kicked a long way and he was leaning over into the great bin to get it but with the earthquake he fell in with the rubbish, a light boy, energetic but skinny.
He guessed it was an earthquake as he'd experienced a few in his time and he hadn't seen the ground moving but he'd felt the rubbish jolt.
When everything stopped he looked over the sides.
Everyone had disappeared.
His friends.
Gone.
Where to?
Home?
But he had the football now.
And he stank so what?
Mama won't approve, though.
He put one foot over the metal then the other foot and he pushed himself off onto stable ground.
Quiet.
And then he realized.
Fear.
He thought he would wait until people showed themselves as they would, in time.
They would come and find him and tell him everything was the same as it always was and will be.
But he was an impatient boy.
They kept telling him he was impatient when he played football, "You don't have to take on the whole team yourself," and, when he was learning for school, "You can't learn all the equations tonight."
He didn't even like sleeping.

The Wooden Tongue Speaks

It seemed like a waste of time.
He would spend most nights awake, fighting warm blankets and sheets, sweating, forcing his eyes to shut and accept sleep.
The love for his patch of land brought him to tears when he pushed opened the door to the apartment block.
He'd done some of the graffiti but nobody knew.
He'd carved into the corner by the letterboxes 'Where is the Future?' and every time he saw it he felt guilty but he had to do it for the dragons in his stomach.
And mama was disgusted with the vandalism.
The stairs smelled of piss.
The lighting was so poor a few old people had hurt themselves.
The elevator broke down with consistency.
When he was a baby, mama took him out in the pram and when they got back one time the elevator violently shook them and when it stopped mama slid open the panel to see concrete.
Mama then shouted for help.
Eventually a neighbor heard and pulled them out.
Since then he'd got stuck by himself.
It was terrifying with the space so limited.
He still had the football under his right arm.
It was a good, heavy football made of strong leather.
It wasn't his but now he had it.
The elevator wasn't a good idea.
It was too risky.
What if the cables snapped due to movement?
He'd crash to the basement and no one would ever find him.
He decided to walk fast up the stairs but what if the earthquake was only taking a break?
Napping, waiting for him to start climbing…
He stopped moving.
He noticed there was dirt on his forearms.
That free kick was great when he tucked it away for they weren't concentrating.
He celebrated and got clipped round the ears.
He wasn't as good at dribbling because he was scared of getting tackled by hard-boned shins.

And he hated passing because it was a waste of time.
What he had to do was get close enough and let someone who couldn't shoot pass to him and then he did his magic, his hard crisp shot the cross-eyed keeper couldn't see.
His team loved it.
It was the miniature World Cup and he was tiny like Maradona.
He didn't have the Great One's skills yet but those skills would come naturally in time.
The boy was always wary of the first floor.
He didn't know anybody there and it seemed a little darker than the other floors and the numbers had faded on the doors.
He never saw the first floor people as he lived on the fourth floor but those people had gone to work.
When they got home late that day they found their crystal smashed on the floor.
Damn these earthquakes!
What if the TV got smashed?
The boy's family was one of the first to get a color television and they celebrated by inviting their neighbors to come and watch the World Cup.
The neighbors brought beers.
They laughed and drank and enjoyed the color, every last hue dancing on their eyeballs.
When it was over they were disappointed and then took their color for granted.
But that family had been one of the first and it was because of their hard work.
Also connections, relations and luck.
It was all getting a bit much for this frail boy.
It'd never been as quiet and total silence was unnatural.
He imagined the walls decomposing.
Bit by bit.
He was scared when he was left by himself at night because his parents were too busy entertaining guests.
But his parents were there, in his home, and they would come if he screamed for them.
Only they wouldn't come.
He was sure of that.

The Wooden Tongue Speaks

In fact he was trembling like a frozen kitten and his legs were like
inanimate rocks.
And he was out of breath.
They won't come.
"Mama!"
Hot tears.

"Tata!"
Even tata will do.

"Mama!"
But mama's better.

Mama will do anything to save her boy.
She loves him.
So does tata.
Despite the fear he thought he would see if his friend's in, his best friend,
who, no matter what anyone says, is not stupid.
He knows what they don't.
He's got a heart of gold and he really cares.
And his stamps and cigarette boxes aren't bad either.
Ring the bell.
Press it hard.
He hears the locks turning and the chains sliding on the other side.
His friend's mother stands there, half-blocking the light, her face twisted
by worry.

"Hello Lucian! Oh my God were you on the stairs when the earthquake
hit?"

"No I wasn't. I was outside."

"Oh good. Thank God! It was horrible. We were holding on to the TV
because it was trying to slide off the cabinet and just imagine what
would've happened then! Running around trying to push the furniture
back in place and I was screaming forget it get to safety!"

Bogdan Tiganov

"Jesus!"
Her eyes dance.

"Go home quickly. Go."

"Ok," and she kisses him on the left cheek and he doesn't even wait for the door to close he's up the stairs forgetting everything, he's up the stairs skipping past the third floor where tata's football friend lives and the light bulb's gone but you're pressing the buzzard, madly knocking and mama opens the door and you hug her with what you've got.
There's tata.
He comes to pick you up.
He wants to give you a slurpy kiss.
There's tataia at the kitchen table.
He laughs that beloved laugh.
That sound can change anything.
Mamaia's gone out for bread.
She's getting milk especially for you.
God knows how long she waits in those queues.
For you.
The kitchen table is where it's always been, in the middle getting in the way of the fridge.
And the balcony's still there, a strong balcony, the concrete tightly woven in to your home.
Everybody's staring at how dirty you are and their voices are like angels chirping down to you.
You are loved.
You go sit in the living room where tata's trying to fix the telly.
He's desperately trying to do that and you know it's best not to disturb him.
Concentrating makes him nervous.
But he smiles at you and asks about the football.

"I hit a great shot."

And you're right.
It's the one thing that sets you apart from the other boys.

The Wooden Tongue Speaks

The power of your shot.
Mama comes in to give you a glass of water.

She tells you "Go and wash. Now!"

Tataia follows her in.
"That was the worst earthquake since 77," he says.

Nobody says anything in reply.
It's the truth.
The wallpaper is gold.
It's magic now the sunshine sweeps in and radiates off the walls.
And the cabinet with its many books, most of them exhilarating.
It's exciting deciding which one to read.
White Fang, your favorite.
You read it in bed where mamaia makes sure you are completely covered,
in bed then where you are boiling hot.
And White Fang in the wild, freezing with hardship.
It makes you appreciate the love you have.
Mamaia's back and mama goes to open the front door for her.
They go to the kitchen and you hear them.

"Where's my beautiful Lucian?"

"He hardly noticed it…"

Don't forget, you were always there at the foundations.
She comes to see you, this woman heading towards old age with the heart
of ten who takes you in her arms, hugging you like nobody else can.
She gives you all her love all the time.

The Children

He went to school once but didn't like it.
He didn't like the children.
They showed off to him.
Here's my new watch.
What do you think of my pencil case?
And they talked about their parents.
Mama's picking me up.
Tata's a martial arts expert.
It was about showing off and saying your parents were best.
Also, the teacher, and the work she presented, was ridiculous.
What was the use of the stuff?
Can you eat literature?
Can you sleep on biology?
Can you live by mathematics?
No, Gavros decided school wasn't for him.
It was for them.

The elders, three men and four women,
made the contrast between them and us clear.
We are poor.
We have nothing.
Nobody cares about us.
They hate us.
They ignore us.
They've thrown us away.
They don't think like us.
We're lucky with what we've got.
They take it for granted.
Actually, two of the women weren't as clear-cut.

The Wooden Tongue Speaks

They don't like us because we're different and we're different because they
don't accept us.
There's no institution for us, not really.
And there's not enough help.
In the evening they sat outside on the steps keeping watch.
If the police come give them their usual.
If anybody else complains tell them where to shove it.
They also kept watch for rival groups, the animals who'd forgotten their
humanity.
It happens.
Often.

So instead the animals snapped their children's limbs or kept the prettiest
ones intact, selling them for sex.
After eleven o'clock the elders went inside gathering the children.
They'd tell them not to play on the streets in darkness.
Ordinary people turned monstrous at night.
They lose their inhibitions.
They want to kill us.
They want to kill anything that might scare them.
They drink too much and their laughter turns to violence.
They talk too much and their words turn to hatred.
You wouldn't believe how an innocent looking old woman can suddenly
stab you in the heart.
The young ones imagined monsters hiding around tree trunks, under cars
and coming out of bars.
These things in their best clothes, clean and happy, smooth-faced.
They will, in an hour, in two hours, turn into beasts.

Everybody went inside and the younger children would go to sleep if
sleep hadn't already taken them.
The older children sat with the elders the other side of the room.
They had fixed chairs to sit on and they talked about what had happened
in the day.
There was usually a lot to talk about and Gavros was thankful to have
excellent friends.
Viviana was one of those, a twelve-year-old girl with terribly pretty

eyes. She liked to tease him and pull on his hair.
It was, admittedly, overgrown.
And Sonia was another great friend.
She was thirteen and smart.
She had an opinion on everything.
She thought that Jesus would come any second to punish everyone.
One of the elders was also his friend.
Simu was Gypsy and his language was elementary.
But he walked like a king and his sense of humor was seen as something to treasure.

If you get up early you catch the world by its balls.
Six o'clock and everybody is awake.
The elders smoked their cigarettes in silence.
The children couldn't wait to get out.
They split into groups.
When you're begging from people in cars you've got to keep your head up because people, most likely, will tell you to go away.
Some will have stronger words to say to you and you've got to keep your cool and move on to the next car.
If it gets too much, if they come out to touch you, you spit in their direction and run off.
That's quite rare though.
It happened once, as far as Gavros could remember.
An old man with heavy hands got out of his black car and slapped him on the back.
It really hurt but he ran away.
Only the man ran after him for a while.
Then he quit because people are gutless.
Gavros went home crying, a big red mark on his back.
Simu saw him and listened.
He didn't smile or joke.
He asked Gavros what the man looked like, what car he was driving, and a couple of days later, in the local news, the journalist reported that a man's house had been set on fire.
Petrol bomb.
Easy to make.

The Wooden Tongue Speaks

Gavros was usually assigned to beg from cars.
He was good at it.
He had a believable grace about him.
He was aging, though, and had to be moved to the market.
And once he started working the market, and the little shops around it, he didn't want to go back to cars because he got to spend a lot of time with Viviana.

"You're the best looking boy I've ever seen."

It was lunch. They were having cheese and mămăligă[10].

"Why don't you kiss me then?"

He looked at her and indeed her eyes were the most beautiful things he'd ever seen.

"I don't love you. I love Petre."
She was so sincere.

"No you don't. He hates you."
Petre was a boy with a reputation.

"You don't know. He's nearly a man!"

"Fuck him," he said and spat down some food.

"Don't talk like that. It's disgusting."

"Yeah, well..."

"But you are the best looking boy."

"Better than Petre?"

"Oh yeah, no problem."

---

10   *Mămăligă is the Romanian equivalent of polenta. It is very much a food of the peasants.*

Bogdan Tiganov

"Then why do you love him? Why don't you love me?"
He looked at her and when he said "love" he felt starved.
He wished he was eating her, inhaling her girly scents.
"Don't worry about it. You're a sweet boy."
She reached over and pulled on his hair.

"Sure, sure, you're wasting your fucking time."

They continued eating, staring at people, staring at streets, staring…
What they had to do was walk around the stalls and wait for customers
then ask them for change.
They had to say "Please."
Some kind shopkeepers, like the baker, always had a bit of bread to give
them.
They put everything in their pockets.
Then they gave it all to the elder, who would be waiting out of sight.
In return the elder would smile and say something nice.
Gavros was no good at it.
He kept hassling people too much, using the same pleading tone as with
cars.
The people were too busy for that.
They were more interested in buying trendy clothes and cigarettes and
Colombian coffee and biscuits.
They were too concentrated on their needs to notice.

"A few coins madam? A few, not much, not a lot…"

And later clutching at their trousers "Come on sir, come on fucker!"

And later no tears, ever.

Fear was in your heart waiting to live.
You had to do what you had to do otherwise you had to accept there's a
beating coming.
So you had to be liked.
You had to rely on your looks to get by and keep your voice nice and

The Wooden Tongue Speaks

sweet.
But it's not like that, you said to yourself, these people are my friends and family and everything I have.

"Stop crying and be a man."
If you look at your shoes long enough everything else starts to fade. Shoes with character, shoes with meaning.

"You'll learn. You have to."

"I know. Leave me alone."

The footsteps moved and it was quiet.
There was no stopping the tears, the sadness, his whole stomach throwing itself up on him.

They left him alone to sit, gave him mămăligă and cheese and he chewed on it while staring through the walls.

"What happened?"

"Nothing. It's the change."

"Oh, the change…"
He lit up.
His hands were dirty brown.

"I don't know if he's up to it."
Simu slapped at a fly.

"We need to…talk about this."

"I've got a feeling it's urgent. I feel maybe he could run."

"He wouldn't. Gavros' not a traitor."

Eventually, he got tired of looking at nothing and feeling sad and he

looked at her smiling with her arm around Petre's waist.
She shone.
He couldn't eat.
She didn't even look at him.
She wasn't interested.
There was something better available to her.
He could get a gun for fifty dollars.
It was simple.
That option was available.
Who would he shoot first?
She wasn't interested.
Viviana was somewhere else, not in the room, not eating and listening.
Where did she come from?
Where was her heart and where was her mind?
What was she made of?
He finished his meal, wiped his mouth with his hand and, with his fingertips, brushed his hair away.
Brigitte Bardot, meanwhile, worried about stray dogs.

★

And yet, when it was bedtime, Viviana came to him and whispered a story in his ear, stirring him, waking him: the master of Darane Swatura[11]

Once upon a time there lived a big family of dogs. It was a curious family. It was very curious because they were all different types of dogs. The mama dog was a black dog with wispy hair. Her hair rose up when things got difficult. The tata dog was yellow, or beige, and he had long ears but he couldn't hear very well. And the puppies, well there were many puppies, so many that not even mama could remember how many.

They lived in a small house. It was small, no matter which side you looked from or how near you got to it. The house was well kept. It was tidy and pretty and it had exactly one room. There was a garden, which

---

[11] *Magical and Superstition stories.*

was also small. Nobody played in that garden because sweeping fields surrounded the house, curves and bumps of light serene green, paths that led to the forest, fields and hills and mountains even. You could play in that and you would never run out of space. And first thing in the morning, when the sun had not yet stretched its arms, there were melodious harmonies in the fields and hills and mountains.

Creanga[12] was a special puppy, special because he was red, so absolutely bright red, blood red. He was also a special puppy because of the way he was. He would carry himself with dignity, always polite, thoughtful, helpful, and neighbors called him Mr Creanga, this red puppy with blue eyes and a nose for what was right.

Sometimes, you could say he was a sad puppy. There was not enough food on the table. There was not enough space to sleep in. But he didn't cry himself to sleep. He knew there was always something better round the corner, the never-ending hills and the early morning music, and possibly the night sky, round and forgiving.

One morning, though, there was no music.

It upset everyone. They kept waiting for the music to come for they didn't know what to do without it. They weren't used to silence. The day couldn't begin otherwise. There would be no work, no learning, there would have to be but it wouldn't be the same.

The tata dog said to the puppies "Don't worry, it will come soon." They believed him. Tata was always right.

The mama dog said "Don't cry, the Gypsies are very tired today."

They listened to her words of wisdom and they felt the tiredness of the Gypsies in their own bones.

---

12 *Ion Creanga (1837/1839-1889) was one of the most famous Romanian writers, famous for his astonishing stories for children. It's also quite astonishing that he said he was born in 1837 whereas historians say he was born in 1839!*

Creanga asked "What if the music will never come again?" This made the other puppies fearful. They trembled and hid behind the garden tools.

The tata dog and the mama dog had no answer. They knew that Creanga was a special puppy, that he burned in their eyes.

They would all just have to wait.

They waited every day. And tata dog worked the garden and fixed the roof but the tiles fell off and wouldn't stick back on. The plants grew viciously and he could no longer keep up with them. The roof wasn't straight, its triangle wasn't as triangular. And mama dog cleaned the house but there were too many spiders in the corners, the spiders multiplied fast, their cobwebs got too sticky and too strong. The food she made wasn't as delicious and she could tell by their disappointed faces. They waited every day.

Creanga told no one of his plans.

It was difficult to find your way out. It was difficult when you were lost. You had to keep to what you knew. The village would begin and end very quickly and the beyond was vast beyond comprehension. Everybody worked hard in that village, some harder than others. He saw them digging and carrying. He saw them taking their humans out to graze. The humans were ugly. Only rarely did he see a human good enough to stroke. He saw them readying the land. The sunflowers were big, bigger and taller than anything, and the wheat smelt so wonderful, old and peaceful.

He kept going to the edge and turning back.

It was too dangerous for a puppy, even a special red puppy like himself.

One day he refused to see and feel the edge.

The Wooden Tongue Speaks

Out beyond was dreamlike. Everything was enormous. The trees made powerful shadows where he walked. There were no houses in those trees, no houses and no birds. Everything was still. Everything was quiet. The shadows kept him cool and he rested for a while. He'd never walked as much before. There was no more path to walk on. The bare trees and hills were not much company. They didn't talk. Only slight murmurs between the leaves but those murmurs made no sense. They weren't interested in him.

He was a stranger there.

After resting he continued having no idea where he was going, lost with no path back. He was starting to feel homesick. He wanted his brothers to play with. He wanted his mama to sing to him like she did when she was happy, but the village was far away, like it had never existed.

He realized how much he loved the village, with its noise and activity, but he stopped and thought to himself 'I must be a brave dog' and he thought 'So what, so what if the sun has disappeared?'

He was a brave dog but he was also a very thoughtful one. He imagined his mama and tata were out looking for him, asking around "Have you seen young Creanga?" and then he turned back. He would find his way, nature would help him, nature wanted to help if you let it. He started running. Then stopped. He'd gone the wrong way you know? This lake was never here before.

It was impossible because it couldn't have been here, a lake like this so long.

He wanted to look at the rocks sticking out from the lake. As he got closer, he saw the lake was clean and its color red. He wasn't sure about the color because the light was dim. The rocks were giant rocks and very sharp. He felt relaxed. He looked at the lake fading away into the distance and he wondered how far it went and how he could get to the end. It really was peaceful and he didn't know why. He started following the right side of the lake, watching how the red water would come so gently over the pebbles. He thought 'I have to go home, but I wish I could stay here and look at this water.'

He felt sleepy. It was late.

Then he heard the sound of metal clacking against metal, slight dings which made his heart jump and his eyes water. He was a brave puppy who loved to play and loved adventure. He listened to the sound which was very clear because there was no other sound. He wanted to go to it but the sound was coming to him. And as he turned he saw a bright yellow illuminated cloth and an incredible mask with horns on top so he fainted.

The masks were hideous and wonderful. All the masks had horns on top, longer or shorter, made out of different materials, like bone or cotton. The masks had hair on the sides or below. They had fur on them and pearls around the eye holes. They were colorful, blue and red and green.

Their costumes were mainly bright yellow, with only the rare dress being red. The costumes had simple decorations and patterns on them, swirls and shells, leaves and drops. He was surrounded by bright yellow when he came round. And there was talking, which he didn't understand, not a word.

What would mama and tata say about this?

Not a word did he understand and they kept talking and talking, trying to explain themselves in their language.

Their sounds got more and more familiar. More and more…

"Red puppy, let us explain to you."

"Red puppy, you have come from the sky."

"Red puppy, the earth made you."

"Let us explain. Darane Swatura."

"Our dearest friend, our beloved brother."

"He is dead, red puppy, he is dead."

"It is a tragedy."

"It is God's will."

"Our dearest friend, the master of Patshivaki Djilia[13]."

"The master of Brigaki Djilia[14]."

"He is dead."

"Koloro is dead."

"God has taken him."

"May he live like a King in heaven."

"Red puppy, let us explain to you."

"Our brother, Koloro, went to the river."

"He went to swim like always."

"He was happy."

"He was the happiest Gypsy in the world."

"And near the river, near the river, red puppy, a man attacked our dear

---

13 *Friendship songs.*
14 *Sorrow songs.*

brother, Koloro."

"He will make even God laugh and cry and sing."

"He was so happy."

"A master of song."

"Red puppy, a man has taken away our music."

"A man has taken away our great friend."

"We cannot live like this."

"It is a sad time."

"Men fear us."

"Men kill us."

"It is tragic."

"But now you are here, red puppy, you."

"You must make the trees wave again."

"The birds sing again."

"The flowers bloom again."

"You."

"Red puppy."

"You must make this happen."

Creanga was confused. He couldn't really understand a word of what they were saying. So many masks…

"But I can't do this! I don't know anything!"

"Don't worry, red puppy."

"You have the magic."

"You have the strength."

"You have the talent."

"You will make the river pure."

"You will make the air like perfume."

Creanga was a brave dog. He wanted to do everything he could to bring the music back.

"What should I do?"

"Listen carefully, red puppy, this will be your making."

"Every day, every morning, you must rise first."

"You leave the house."

"And you walk."

"And you see."

"And you listen."

"And you feel."

"You touch."

Bogdan Tiganov

"You clean your eyes and ears."

"Then you create stories."

"Stories like songs."

"Stories that grow from the ground."

"Stories which reach the sky."

It sounded wonderful but he had no idea how to make stories or how to sing stories!

"How will I create these stories? How will I sing these stories?"

"You do not."

"Just let them grow."
"And come to us."

"Come to us when you're ready."

"Take this collar and wear it."

"Mirella made it for you with all our love."

"The collar will take you here."

"When you're ready."

"When the stories have grown."

He took the collar, which was yellow with a red line woven across it.

"Go, red puppy, you are late."

He didn't want to go.

"You are very late."

"You must go."

"But we will see each other soon."

"Very soon."

"Mountains do not meet but we do."

They led him back to the village and he was so very tired, almost asleep, almost, and he walked home afraid of what was to come.

The house was very small, it was incredibly small, the smallest house he'd ever seen, his home. Inside, they had been waiting.

They had been crying but they jumped up, electrified, when they saw him enter.
He wasted no time. He told them not worry, that he'd found the Gypsies and that everything was going to be like it was, maybe better.

And they laughed and laughed then fell asleep, so tired and relieved.

The following morning Creanga awoke determined. He went out and smelt the wheat. He went out and watched the humans, he watched the birds, he watched the pigs, he watched the cows. He listened to their talk, their happiness and unhappiness. He felt the tomatoes, he felt the radishes, ate an apple or two.

At the end of the day he had not yet learned the secret but he felt like he was learning something.

A year later, first thing in the morning, when the sun had not yet stretched its arms, Glassoor Mode[15] washed over the hills and

---

15 *Fun and Dance songs. All terminology taken from a great site on Romany names and culture:* *www.miniclan.org/pathrell/romany.html*

mountains and fields. It was so joyous the whole village awoke in a hurry and went outside to listen. It was like nothing they had ever heard before. It wiped the sleep from their faces and gave them determination. Their smiles greeted the sunshine.

Mama and tata and all the puppies, the entire village no doubt, were so proud of their red puppy who had become the master of Darane Swatura.

He had been asleep for a while, buried in shadow, snoring and turning from time to time. And, yet, she had continued with her story. She had finished, now. Eyes sparkled in the darkness.

It's Marlboro

There were two of them, one slighter older, and they had a job to do.
The job involved waiting for people to come and then ring the cemetery bell.
When they saw people coming they would walk up to the rope and tug on it and tug on it, not too long, just enough.
The people were usually old women who nodded their head in approval.
The bell made them feel they were entering a holy place.
It was a symbol.
It meant something.
Sometimes they would forget to stop.
The bell just kept ringing.
The job also involved going to clean the graves and tombs.
The slighter older one didn't want to do it.
He would say he'd done enough of it.
The younger one also didn't want to do it.
He just didn't want to.
And so they had to rely on a young kid who'd somehow drifted in there.
The kid would do it.
He was a good boy.
You would say kid go and do it and before you'd finished he'd be there doing it.
The kid went to the graves where no one was.
He liked to be out of the way.
He liked to do his job and go back quickly without being noticed.
His job was to clean the graves.
It was to wash them which meant throw some water on them.
It was to arrange the plants which meant don't let the plants grow over the grave.
But the problem was the size of the place.

Bogdan Tiganov

Too many graves for one boy.
So some were clean and some weren't.
In fact none were clean because he couldn't throw the water properly and he was afraid of getting stung by the overgrown plants.
Of course he was seen, and he didn't like that.
He didn't like to feel their eyes watching him, measuring him, watching him, these sorrowful people, these sad people with their tears and memories in black clothes.
Black clothes against gray/green trees and gray/white/blue sky and the distance.

What was that distance beyond the cemetery?
He didn't know, this boy, but he found his eyes being drawn to that distance.
He couldn't take his eyes back and put them on the job.
His eyes weren't listening, too busy looking far.

"Work boy."
That was the only memory of his mother.
She'd said that.

"Don't waste your time."
He wasn't sure she'd said that but it made sense as it forced him to clean the graves.
Work was important.
Work was what he had to do.
Everything else worked.
All the creatures worked.
The plants worked.
Even his friends worked, ringing the bell.
He didn't like them.
They rang the bell.
Did they think that was enough?
Did they deserve to have a roof over their heads and a meal on their laps and a drink near their lips for ringing the bell?
Maybe that's how work goes.
You start off cleaning the graves and you end up ringing the bell.

The Wooden Tongue Speaks

You get older and you can't bend your back to cut the plants or sweep the leaves off.
He tried to understand them.
They were good people.
They didn't beat him.
They didn't swear at him.
They drank too much, if not all the time, but they were used to it.
And he'd gotten used to the smell.
It was nothing.
In the evening they'd sit in their hut.
The hut had very few things inside, a bunk bed, a single bed, a couple of religious pictures on the walls and the television.
There were no windows, only the small black and white television which they stared at.
The picture was very bad on the television.
They were watching the world ice-skating championship.
The boy couldn't believe how graceful, elegant and heart-stopping the little people on the television were.
He could really feel with them when they hit the ice with their bottoms.
Even that was exciting.

"Hey I've got a cigarette I've been saving," said the older one.
He looked old but he wasn't older than fifty.

"Great," said the slightly younger one.

"It's Marlboro."

A kind woman had given him a whole pack of Marlboro a month earlier.

"I know."

"It's Marlboro. Do you understand?"

"Yes. Where is it?"

Bogdan Tiganov

And the older one fumbled through his colorless garments, fumbled and fumbled until he found the cigarette, bent and old but useful.

"I don't have a light," said the slightly younger one.

"Me neither," said the slightly older one.

"Kid, do you have a light?"
The boy, his eyes were fixed on the television.
Captivated.

"Kid? A light?"
The boy couldn't take his eyes off the beauties,
beautiful beautiful princesses.
He was falling in love with every-one of them.
He didn't have a light.

"Kid, do you have a light or not?" and the older one got up and switched off the television.
The boy looked at him.

"I don't," and the older one switched it back on.

"Where are we going to get a light?" somebody said later and they were all quite drunk.

"I don't know…I don't know."

"We need a light."

"We do."

"I'll get the light," said the boy.
He wondered why he'd said that.
It was warm in there.
He was sleeping but their voices woke him and he felt their voices were putting pressure on him so he had to say it, but now he was outside and

The Wooden Tongue Speaks

it was cold and dangerous.

Close by to the cemetery was a row of houses, worn to the extremes,
angled downwards, houses that seemed to shrink unnaturally.
The boy knew the aging inhabitants well as they spent a great deal of time
crouched over graves, whispering personal prayers.
He came to the first house.
It was built on a slope and sinking, a house where an old blind woman
lived.
She was very well liked but nobody cared about her, not even her son,
who was an alcoholic.
He could feel the danger more.
The street gangs had no mercy.
They would knife you and beat you if they caught you where you didn't
belong.
They were strong and they were fast.
They hated you before seeing you.
They had bony faces and devilish eyes.
Around this corner.
They'd caught him many times.
He had scars.
The boy knocked on the door.
He was afraid.
Maybe she'd died.
Maybe he was the one who'd find her dead with her mouth open and her
eyes blank and her arms extended towards the sky.
That's where God is and he's waiting for me.
He'd heard her say that.

"Yes!"

"I'm sorry...I know it's very late."

"Is it? I was sleeping. What's the time?"

"I don't know...I need a light."

Bogdan Tiganov

"Pardon?"

"A light! A lighter! A match!"

"Who are you?"

"I'm the boy from the cemetery. We've talked before."
"What? What did we talk about?"

"I can't remember."

There was a pause, like she'd gone off somewhere.
"I don't have a light."

"Then how do you light your oven?"

"I don't have a light."

"I'm your son, I need a light."

"You're not my son. I don't know you."
Her tone was unsure.

"Go away. I need to sleep."

"I'm your son, open this door now!" and when he shouted the next-door
light went on.
He saw it in the window, panicked and started running, running down the
street and turning right, nearly falling over in a large hole.
He found himself with a cut on his right shin.
There must've been a sharp rock.
Now what?
Where do you go?
The neighbors are awake and they're searching everywhere for you.
Where is that boy?
Let me put a bullet between his eyes.
He ran a little further.

The Wooden Tongue Speaks

It was cold and the cold made him forget.
The boy saw a man drinking in the street.
He was an old man.
He avoided the old man.
He wanted to rob the old fool but he didn't have it, guts.
The ghost of Panait Istrati had always kept an eye out for a true soul and now he had his eye on the boy.
What he's been through!
How he deserves something else!

The door made a severe sound.
They had finished the alcohol and were asleep, almost hugging each other.

"Hey! I have the light!" said the boy and pulled out a green lighter from his right pocket.

They didn't move.

"Wake up! Look!" and he went to them and shook them with all his strength, he shook like hell and nothing.

"Alright," and he went outside.

He pulled on the rope with what he had left, he pulled on that rope which had frozen over.
It made a good strong sound.
Crows lifted themselves from branches, flew over into the distance.
They came out and grabbed him and the slightly younger one punched the boy.
The boy was out.
They made sure the bell was ok but the bell kept ringing.
Something was wrong with it.

"What next?" asked the slightly older one as blood poured out his mouth.
He was dying.

Bogdan Tiganov

"Look at that," said the slightly younger one and they looked at the boy who had smoke coming out of his head.

"He's on fire."

In the Mind

The man upstairs is digging a hole through the ceiling.
He starts digging when everyone, and I mean everyone, is asleep.
Sometimes I can see his eye.
His eye watching me, waiting for me to undress.
He blinks and pretends he's not there and even when I stare at him, with all the hatred I possess, he still does not feel an overwhelming need to disappear.
He knows that nobody is aware of what's going on and, because of that, I am helpless.
Therefore, I sleep with my clothes on.
And I wait long enough for the noise to abate.
The lights are, at times, blinding, like driving at night when headlights seem sun-bright as if they're doing it on purpose.
Maybe they are doing it on purpose turning and blasting whatever they've got, shop lights, apartment lights, lamps, lampposts and torches, a few candles in the church magnified by windows.
What does it all mean?
I watch them for hours until they blow out.

They're not awake yet.
I couldn't sleep much.
I couldn't sleep.
I must be suffering from insomnia, also.
I kept seeing them coming.
I kept seeing and disbelieving.
I hear the neighbor beating his wife most nights.
Nobody else hears this.
Nobody else knows what's going on next door.
And sometimes the screams are very soft, as if she's gotten used to it

Bogdan Tiganov

and feels no need to scream.
That scares me most.
Somebody can become so used to their punishment they can no longer scream.
I am like that, though, sitting here, near the window, voiceless.
If you ask me I won't answer.
You disgust me and I want nothing to do with you but, at the same time, I love you and I can't imagine being anywhere else.
Who knows where I would be if I had been alone in times of need.
Dead.
My hands shake involuntarily and the cigarette hangs from my lips like a pastiche to film noir.
Maybe that is what I am or have become.
A picture.
A memory.
I don't really want to exist.
It is inconvenient when I am being prodded.
I don't prod you so why prod me?
Just let me tremble here.
Even where you are not behind me I see you watching me, analyzing me, disgusted with the way I am.
You think I am lazy and every time you see me you want to swear at me or destroy me.
My eyes hurt.
My eyes hurt from the light.
I hear you.
I hear you.
But I don't feel you.
You could try slapping me very hard.
My head will shake and my hair will flop like it does and hang over.
Hey, you say.
Hey, you say and click your fingers as if you could bring me back.
Do you think I would jump from this balcony?
I have never thought of jumping.
People can't fly.
They can, on the other hand, go splat.
I like to hear the tram go by.

The Wooden Tongue Speaks

It is one of my favorite sounds.
Calming.
I like the horn sounding like something vital.
Deadly.
Immediate.
Then the sound of the wheels on the track, creaking slightly, fades.
I like seeing the small kids play, especially the ones with the woolly hats, red and blue, black and blue, woolly hats too big for their delicate little heads.
I love watching them play, how their motor functions aren't quite perfect, how they miss and, sometimes, fall over.
I don't like to hear them wailing.
I hate knowing they're unhappy, that somehow they think they've failed.
I can't breathe when it happens.
Don't ever have children until you're ready.
But is that how we were built?
Were we built to be ready?
Everything is about timing.
Time this.
Time that.
Get to work early or on time.
Have your lunch-break.
Come back on time.
Go home.
Eat.
Make sure the alarm clock is right.
And make sure you wake up on time.
The right time is when you're ready.
I like to watch the birds falling from the sky out of the corner of my eye.
They never rise again.

When they all leave it is quiet.
I hope the phone won't ring, the house phone or mobile.
The way I'm feeling, the way it's all going today, I can't handle rings as the sounds may paralyze me with fear.

Bogdan Tiganov

Who are they looking for anyway?
Mama?
Tata?
Me?
Are they looking for me?
What can they possibly want from me?
A broken lipstick?
A pair of tights?
In here I used to sit and listen to bunica's[16] stories as she brushed my hair.
She used to brush it and tell me what it was like many years ago.
Why did she tell me all those stories?
All those personal stories?
And how much of it was lies?
How many lies have I accepted?
Swallowed like a pill, this pill, that pill, all pills are supposed to make you happy.
People generally treat me like a doormat.
Or maybe she loved me and thought I wanted to hear her stories.
Were those stories good for me?
Did they make me believe in the goodness of others or the absolute evil of circumstance?
What about the love she received in the end?
Was it enough to wrap up her life in the way she deserved?
Was she satisfied or was she broken?
I want to bounce on this bed but I can't.
My body feels too heavy and it's weighing down the fabric.
I want to move a bit.
And rock up and down.
Or rock out like in the clubs.
But this body of mine won't allow it.
You think I don't feel anything.
Instead, I feel too much.
I feel rejection like a burden.
I feel happiness like a hypothesis.
When you shout I feel like you're boring a hole through my stomach.
You find me at my worst.

---

16 *Romanian for Grandma.*

The Wooden Tongue Speaks

You find me when I want to hide.
You see me motionless, thoughtless and blank.
What must you think of me?
I want to sleep.
And when you're not here and I can't hear a thing and I can calm this narrator, that being you, you, you, you...
Do you remember when they took you down into the cellar?
And do you remember when they locked you in a cell with another psychologically disturbed individual who sat opposite you crying?
Do you remember that?
Because if you do it's probably a good sign.
You were so agitated...
You couldn't stand to look at the mattress, that cold thing with the springs which dug into your sides when you gave up and curled up.
Sometime during the night you awoke to find this creature, this beast with dark eyes staring down at you.
It was mama.
Or tata.
Or it could've been the all-knowing eyes of Jesus.
But you will never know because you were so frozen, literally as well as fearfully, that you closed your eyes and forced them to stay shut even though it hurt and you thought death was staring at you.
Then when you woke up you realized that you had wet yourself and you wanted to go somewhere but you didn't trust anybody and you felt reality disintegrating.
Do you remember what it was like the following day?
Their assessment?
They didn't know what was wrong with you or what had happened to you.
They were guessing.
Stammering.
It was pathetic and your eyes were darting around like a rabbit in the headlights.
The lights.
Yes.
Why were the walls painted bright white?
To blind you?

Bogdan Tiganov

I go through my stuff.
All the stuff you don't touch because you're afraid of what you'll find.
You might find a piece of me that you would prefer to forget.
I find a Nouvelle Vogue album that I used to love when I was a teenager.
It's on tape and I take it with me to the living room where I put it on the
old stereo system.
I sit on my knees.
"That's right you did say nothing and yet you told me everything –
through your eyes, through the way you stared at me when you saw me.
You didn't recognize me.
You still don't.
Yes, what's left is my childhood and how when you went away we had no father and
when you came back we felt we were invincible.
Give me the words, give me the words so I can make you see who I am.
Sacrificed? What would you know about sacrifice?
You sweet-sounding pampered singer…what would you know?
Saying nothing…give me your words, your true words, the ones that I am not deaf to."

When the song is over I play it again and I imagine myself bullied.
I see myself as a great victim while the pain in my knees worsens.
I take the tape out and put it back where I found it
(in my bedside cabinet)
and I don't bother with anything else as I am tired.
Very.

They tell me it's dinnertime and it takes me awhile to realize where I am.
And who I am.
I hear them calling me.
With anger in their voice.
When I see them they don't say anything.
They've given up on talking to me.
Not enough great answers.
Not fast enough.
And they don't even look up to acknowledge me any longer.
Instead, they stare at me when I sit.
I don't want to sit here like in a museum so I stuff the food down my

The Wooden Tongue Speaks

throat in several fast gulps.
Don't keep staring at me.
I know I'm not supposed to eat like this.
You start talking.
You start saying something which no longer makes any sense to me.
Because I am only aware of my own voices.
Your voices no longer interest me.
They're not relevant to me.
The clock ticks time to our thoughts and feelings.
Yes, I know what you're talking about.
Your jobs, your money, your problems.
You don't really talk about anything else.
And when you try to it's false and you feel like a fraudster and you give up on difference, preferring what you talk of/think of best.
But now the difference is that you don't include me in those conversations. I am outside of your norm.
So you have nothing to talk to me about.
You can't even be bothered to try.
Why?
The best thing to do is to leave them.
The best thing is to never come back.
And maybe tomorrow, if I can leave this place, I may feel I need not come back.
I am not a dog.
I am not tied to you.
I cannot keep waiting and waiting like this.
In the dark.
If the neighbor wants to rape me he should just do it.
Because he wants to do it anyway.
And if all the other men, that unexpectedly stop by, want to fuck me they should just hurry up and do it.
Let's not pretend any longer.
The game we play every day and night has, don't you think, dragged on too long.
I will not take it.
I will not be abused, misused, thrown around like a rag doll, threatened and left to clean up my own tears.

Bogdan Tiganov

My neck is stiff – I feel like I've been digging up and paving streets.
While I'm feeling sorry for myself the real goings-on are about to begin.

Yogurt

It got me started.
I was alive.
I was dead.
I could see myself being born.
I tried to forget many times where I came from and what I had done or not done but I kept remembering and not forgetting quite enough like a cool strawberry on the devil's lips.
The first time was sour like medicine so many doctors so much advice.
They came and gave.
Around me like arrows like hawks like ten Jesus Christs.
It begins with the eternal mystery.
Was it the skin? Was it the meat?
I loved it like an obsession, every day, every morning.
It's healthy, man what isn't?
Have this, it will do good.
Read this and feel better.
And when you feel so great tell everybody else how you got there.
Please. Tell me.
An obsession is an obsession is an obsession.
Like love, like mountain air that you've never had before.
Try it, it's available, and legal illegal it's what we made it and as long as we made it accept it, swallow it.
But it's too late, believe me when you realize you can't change what you've done.
Like birth.
Believe me, everything's like birth.
This yogurt I hang on to.

Bogdan Tiganov

I have it at lunch, when I'm breaking, I'm hoping it will rub off its health on me and leave me on a deserted island where I have no idea what I'll do.

A Father

The daylight seemed like it could go on for a very long time.
It felt that way.
It felt like you could pray all you like but the daylight would keep coming
and you couldn't sleep yet.
You couldn't close your eyes and forget it.
You couldn't.
Nobody could.
Not with the daylight parading its translucent wings over your rooms.
And the birds are dead.
They haven't been singing lately,
not that you tried listening.
They're probably hiding.
The dogs are hiding and there's not enough for them or you.
They smell bad.
They could smell worse.
There's a smell you won't ever forget.
Eat the cats,
there's plenty of them mating under the midnight sky,
all bloody whiskers and savage eyes.
The savage eyes frighten you more than you will let yourself believe.
Still, it will never happen.
It will never get so late.
Not with the daylight pacing around like a wild horse.
The insane have stopped pacing,
kick in the drugs,
let them lie one on top of another mouths agape.
There's one more scream they couldn't quite form.

Bogdan Tiganov

That's insanity for you,
knee deep in piss,
unwashed,
dirty.
This one can't make it to where it needs to go,
it can't make it and there's no one here,
no cameras,
no eyes,
no consciousness.
Only walls and grates,
metal and concrete,
metal and metal,
concrete and concrete,
brick and white paint,
white paint fading.
Not even a spider,
not even a rat,
not even a moth,
not even a soul,
not even a breath,
concrete and metal.
You can't hear the tears flow or drop but they're crying.
They're crying so much they've forgotten how not to.
They're crying for days, months and years.
Decades and centuries.
Centuries of tears,
they're crying now with the concrete and metal,
lifeless cries,
small sobs under the midnight sky.
They tried screaming:
"Help me, help me, oh dear God please help me,
help me God, please God, help me,
mama, tata, brother, sister,
bunicu[17], bunica, please God help me!"
then they stopped talking and they stopped hoping,
their hearts went down,

---

17 *Romanian for Granddad*

The Wooden Tongue Speaks

their stomachs bruised by the countless times they've tried to escape,
no way out son, no way.
Then small sobs will do, pressing against the cold wall.
There where you are or anywhere,
pressing skin against concrete.
Small sobs no one will hear anyway.
Sobs against the sides of faces,
down noses,
eyelashes drunk with sobs.
The tear-ducts are open tonight and every night.
Lights off.
Turn it off.
No "Goodnight."
No "Thank you."
No "Take care."
No need.
Turn it off.
Lights off.
Turn it off.
Let's move on.
Let's go home.
Let's feed the babies.

"I love you mama."

"I love you too."

Let's go home.
Let's drive home.
Let's bus.
Let's train.
Let's tram.
Wake up still night,
finish up still night.
Don't think, don't ever think again, let's go.
Let's go home,
open the doors,

Bogdan Tiganov

open the windows,
clean the floors,
wash the clothes,
brush the teeth,
smoke cigarettes,
drink and drink.
Vodka and beer.
Smoke.
Make the bed,
draw the curtains,
let's go home and kiss,
let's go home and argue.
If you see lights in the windows at midnight,
if you get the chance,
if you see the lights,
it's you and me shouting.
Shadow puppets shouting till we can't shout any more
and the neighbors are pounding on the floor
and shouting at us.
Then everybody's shouting.
It's quiet.
Absolutely quiet.
Only not so,
the cats screech mating,
bloody whiskers everywhere.
Dogs are dying under the midnight sky.
Half-closed eyes,
you're so tired,
unbelievably you got through.
You made it here to where you are.
Where are you?
You don't know and you can't see,
half-closed eyes,
you can't see any more,
you just look there at that point
while bats flap their wings down these corridors.
Christ.

The Wooden Tongue Speaks

Christ waits on the cross.
You don't know about that,
you just look at that point over and over,
that point with half-closed dead blurred vision.
And the bats flap,
flap to prick any unpricked nerves.
And the dogs yelp,
howling,
no moon,
it's light,
so brilliantly light,
how divine,
no moon,
no stars,
trees snap across each other,
trees touch and depart,
trees meet and separate.
Golden leaves,
white white leaves,
white leaves and golden leaves and red leaves waiting,
golden leaves from nowhere,
bats flap their wings across the hall,
everything's trying to climb the plants on the walls,
not strong enough,
cats and dogs and mice and rats and the nameless,
the unknown,
everything's trying to climb these plants by the window.
You can't hear that.
It's just a breeze,
a friend's whisper,
a lover's breath on your neck,
not even a lover,
not even a memory,
these memories cracking,
smashing,
ferociously demolished,
cracking,

Bogdan Tiganov

smashing,
in golden pieces,
floating and drifting down like silent leaves,
meeting and separating.
The lights won't die,
none of them will,
they live so well,
dangling and shining,
they won't die,
the lights illuminating,
the lights showing up,
the lights over here,
friendless and deathly,
deaf,
empty,
hollow,
the lights over here in circle,
in rectangles,
in impossible angles slicing up floors and grounds and earth,
over boxes,
over the midnight sky,
over dead birds and dead dogs and dead cats and dead rats and nothing
breathes,
just the light,
just this illumination,
with the angles slicing.
The doors are closing,
some louder than others.
The footsteps are entering.
Put your feet on the bed,
put them on the sofa,
switch on TV,
food,
eat,
drink,
smoke,
food,

The Wooden Tongue Speaks

eat,
food,
eat,
they want the whole world to know what's in their pot:
onion, garlic and pork.
You can't smell that.
The light chases that away.
There's not enough anger,
there's nothing left,
there's not enough kill,
there's not enough,
there's not enough of anything for anybody.

He'd carried his father on his back.
His father was a big man, heavy from years of drinking.
He could see his father's face but he tried not to look at it.
He kept taking breaks along the way
and there were people who tried to help,
but he said "No,
don't worry about me,
let me do what I must."
So he dragged himself with his father on his back.
He thought he could feel his father's breath on his face
but it was the illusion of wind,
because his father was dead.
He could feel his father's lead-like arms dropping
and smacking down across his back,
so many years laboring,
so much drinking and misery.
He'd hated his father.
He'd loved him too.
His father the monster.
His father the angel.
And he loved him now, dead on his back.
He could hear people preparing their gossip.
Guess what I saw last night?
Guess whom I saw?

Bogdan Tiganov

These parasites.
He concentrated on the task.
His father gained in weight by the second,
nothing was as heavy as this,
sometimes he was on his knees,
then he would rise.
He saw his wife.
He saw his wife crying.
But he could no longer see so well.
She tried to help.

But he said
"No, let me do what I must"
and he pushed her off.

He pulled his father up,
the thud of chest against back.
One more step,
one more,
that's what's left.
He felt his father's skin and his father's hair
and he remembered and tried to forget
and he remembered and he tried to forget,
but he kept remembering the nurses saying
how they'd just leave his father dead there for days
because they had no ambulance to take his father home,
and he said
"I'll take him"
and the nurse said
"Are you crazy?"
and he said
"Yes I'm crazy, I'll take him home."

His wife pushed open the door.
He came in,
his father a mountainous lump of clay,
but he didn't feel anything,

The Wooden Tongue Speaks

there was no pain,
there was no clarity.

"Clear the table"
he said
and his wife brushed everything off it,
the cloth,
the bread,
the water.

He grabbed his father by the waist and lifted him onto the table.
You're home.
Then he fell on the floor.
His wife came to him,
but he said
"No, let me lie here like this,
this is what's become of me."
So she left, weeping.

His daughter came in but his wife took her away.

You're home, tata,
where you felt best,
where you lived,
where you drank,
where you ate your favorite salami and cheese,
and you had wine
which you abused
and which abused you,
you're here tata
and nothing else matters in this world.

The Old Man's Village

The bus drew up into a ditch throwing the passengers' midriffs forward.
Then the driver peeled himself off his seat, popped a peanut in his mouth, bashed open the door and jumped out.
Several people stood up, holding a bag or two or even a broom.
The old man waited and sighed hearing the bus driver stroll by outside humming a football song.
He waited for the passengers to go.
On the slow, burning, journey he hadn't said much.
The sun, on the other hand, had fired off his thinking.
And memories.
Regrets.
The sun had pasted his eyes back with white light, greased his hair, stuck the shirt to his back and made him reach for his plastic bottle of water.
'This water is from my well,' he thought while drinking, 'and it's the best water in the world.'
The old man wasn't simply boasting to himself but merely affirming the truth.

'Can't stay long…must rush back…what will happen to the buffalo? Who's going to collect the honey? Nobody. That's who. Nobody.'

He had these dialogues with himself when he had nothing to do but wait for something.
One of the old women in front attempted to speak to him, having seen him staring, like a poet, out of the window to the hills and prairie.

The Wooden Tongue Speaks

"Have you got family in Huta?" she asked smiling, as old women do when they start.

There was no answer, though.
"I said do you have brothers or sisters in Huta?" she asked, thinking that his hearing's probably not so good.
The old man shifted his gaze.

"I was a servant in Huta. Sixty years ago on Zadic's land!" and when he chuckled she joined him.

"And why are you going there now?"

"Well…" he said, thinking, "I want to see it again."

"Really…"

He scratched the back of his head and, when doing so, his cap slid forward making him look far younger and his eyes said 'This is not the end.'

It was an extremely warm day and it had been like this many years ago but maybe not even then.
It had never been as hot as the day when the old man stooped off the bus and stepped onto the dusty main road in the village of Huta.
He had not appreciated the weak breeze from the bus roof or the flittering shadows because now he had no shade and no wind and he tugged at his cap.
Seeing a house across the road he began walking to it, surprised by the village slumber.
But he thought 'They're out working in the field' and then realized the house wasn't finished as the bricks were randomly piled up and he could see from one side of the house to the other.
The bus driver, or some other man, was outside a place, leaning with his elbow against a table.
That man was drinking from a bottle so the old man grabbed his own bottle and took a big swig of clean, thrilling water.

Bogdan Tiganov

Once more he tugged at his cap and then began moving towards what was once the center.
He moved steadily and not once did he feel like an old man.
When he passed the bar he didn't even look to see if the bus driver was the bus driver.
He kept looking at the houses.
Small.
Demolished.
Unfinished.
And where had his fellow travelers disappeared to?
Nothing going on and quiet just like up on the hill with the cows where sometimes he heard a branch slap another branch, or a wasp dizzy from trying, or God, but, mostly, He was silent.
And where were the porches?
Not one had he seen thus far and not one of these houses had been in such desolate a state when he was a boy.
He heard clearly the galloping horse as the master rode in accompanied.

"Don't stand there like an idiot! Untie my shoes. You will see plenty of horses from now on!"

The master, with his goatee beard and a voice that could make a fully grown man relieve himself, was right as the boy then spent a great deal of time working in the stables, eventually making horseshoes.
But no, there were no horses.
Only the bus, slanted.
A girl showed up in a window but she dashed off too.
'When it rains they face a hard time here,' he thought, caught up in a groove in the dirt, dust spraying over him.
He kept walking, though, because he couldn't stop, feeling the bristles of his beard sprouting in protest against sweat and endless dust.
At the crossroad he stopped.
Here was where he imagined he'd end the journey, near the market where the people would welcome him.
In reality, the market and the people had been replaced by a big oak that had grown crooked while the road ahead went nowhere and to the right a few houses here and there were specks on the hill.

The Wooden Tongue Speaks

And there were no animals or voices to be heard.
The old man stared again at the oak and reminisced…he thought he'd never be able to afford any of the luxurious fruit on sale never mind the fancy clothes he knew not the names of.
He hadn't been able to observe too long then and now that he was a man, and had lived a life, he wanted to stay, take it in and believe he'd earned his place amongst the living and in the eyes of God.
Who would've thought that a tree would overshadow all that?
Natural but out of place, if he could go home he would and bring back with him the axe.
Afterwards, he would not take the logs for winter.
He'd leave them there, scattered, in disgust.
But he couldn't go home for he had plenty of time, what with the bus heading back in five hours or so.
The old man would find out where the people had gone to, whether they had formed a dwelling underground or blown like ashes skyward.
Drinking some more of his water he thought
'I'll go knock on the first door I see.'
While knocking he heard light footsteps on the other side.
An old woman, wearing a red headscarf, opened the door.
She had been on the bus right near the front.

"Come in," she said and stepped back into a dark room where he followed.
In this room, candles showed up the corners and yellow made blue green.
To the side the old man heard a different woman breathing.

Then he felt something prodding his legs.
"Here. Sit down."

It was a chair.
He pulled up his trousers slightly, as he did out of habit, and sat, his eyes adjusting.
In front of him was a bed on which two old women lay.
He tapped his feet on the floor.
Clay.
One of the old women was so small she looked like she had shrunk to

Bogdan Tiganov

fit just half the bed.

"We're sisters," said the slightly larger one who'd opened the door.

"Hmm…"

"What'd you come here for?" asked the small one.
"Oh, you know…"

"Out on a trip are you?"

"No," he said, trying to think and fighting to see.

"What did you work?"
"I was a servant for Zadic. Sixty years ago…or sixty-three…"

"Oh."

"Everybody's gone. After his death, Zadic's children sold everything, absolutely everything, and left."

"Offf…there's only a few of us left," whispered the small one.

The brothers, sisters and cousins of the remaining few would come to visit, sometimes bringing essentials, always bringing gossip.

"We moved after the war."

"Which one?" asked the old man, coyly.

"She went," began the small woman, "and I told her to go!"
Just go! I said.
I could see then the roads were never going to reach us.
How the bus gets here I don't know…" and she trailed off, tired.
The old man tapped his feet on the clay floor, his shoes making reassuring sounds.

The Wooden Tongue Speaks

"I know that. I can see it," he said and shook his head.

"Where's your family?"

"This is it," said the larger woman.

"Nelu's in Spain and Arghil does construction in Italy. Their children are there too…they come, you know, maybe once a year, maybe twice a year, and they don't stay long. They look around. They talk to us. But they don't look like they're home. They don't look the same."

"Arghil," continued the small woman, "is building a villa not far away. He says we'll all live in it. Me! That's what I need…and my daughter can't do a thing. She can't cook, complains about cleaning…her husband does everything…"

"I know," said the old man, his face serious, trying to make out the intricate shapes of the women, "mine are like that."
Silence filled in the gaps.

They analyzed each other and thought about the nights in which they went to bed early because they didn't have anything else to do and it was quiet, like this, and they gave up and slept.
The limbs are tired but the mind is active!

"Have a drink of water," said the larger woman, getting up and then bending over to grab a metal canister from under the bed.

"No, no. I've got water," said the old man, showing her his almost finished bottle.

"Have you eaten?

"Oh…it's not important…"

"What do you mean it's not important? Let me bring you some of our mămăligă from morning…"

and without waiting for his answer she hurried out slamming the door behind.

He could hear the small woman's slightly hoarse breathing. 'She must be ill,' he thought and tried to look at the walls but he could see the blanket covering her. He then looked at his own shoes and shirt.

"I was wondering," he said, smiling, "what's happened to Ion, the son of Meșter? He and I-"

"He's dead."

"Oh."

'Pity.'

"What about Murgu Augustin? We went bathing together in-"

"He's dead too."

'All the old boys…'

"And Costică, his brother? He was fast that boy-"

"He's been dead longer than the other two."

'And I'm still alive!'

"Really? I thought he would live forever," said the old man and exhaled a throaty laugh.

"No one lives forever. Apart from the Communists," and the old woman laughed along too.

"And what about Nucu Aurica? Is she dead?" She was the most beautiful of girls, the angel of the village, God's

The Wooden Tongue Speaks

miracle.

"Aurica? You mean the girl who used to live near the public gardens?"

"That's right."

"You mean the girl who couldn't stop teasing all the stupid boys?"

The old man had tears in his eyes because he had felt her in his heart years after he had gone back home.
Then she gradually began to vanish from his mind and other worries took over.
And now he had remembered.

"You mean the girl with the most delicately embroidered dresses?"

"Yes."

"That girl? Aurica?"

"Hmm…"

"You found me,"
and when she spoke those words the old man's eyes shot up.

He had known that something was a little strange about this place with the yellow blue green lights, clay floor and no windows.
He had known that his life would open out to him like a flower and be crushed beneath the weight of time.
He had known it when he arrived, when he walked in, when he saw the tree, when he followed the red scarf, when he sat on the chair, when he was blind, when all he could see was sadness, he had known it this old man who could feel much more than anyone had realized.

"What…"

"What happened? Yes, what happened? When and how did it happen?

Bogdan Tiganov

And, most importantly, why?"

"I don't know…we…we…"
the old man stumbled and felt his feet weightless and the weight from his feet and the rest of his body an anvil on his mind.

"I thought I recognized the walk but I didn't know from where," said Aurica. "Is that you, Petrică?"

But he hadn't recognized her.
She was just a little old woman, so tiny she had almost no presence.
And now she had become a shadow, illuminated across the walls.
He couldn't breathe.
'What's wrong with this weather?'
The heat had tied a knot in his throat and another knot in his stomach and was pulling on both.

"You're-" but Petrică stopped, hearing the now familiar footsteps.

"Come,"
said the old woman with the red headscarf,
"the table is outside."

⭐
An Interview

She called me on my mobile while I was at work.
I answered, hoping.

"Come at six, Darina," she said,
"and wait outside. There'll be others too."

A whole bunch of people were there.
All women.
Nobody talked and there was no sense of organization.
I was worried somebody else who'd come after me would go in first and everyone shared my worry.
We waited outside a polished metal door near a dirty, unkempt, staircase and other people, people who probably lived close by, would pass and I tried not to look at them.
I don't mind standing, though, especially when it's standing for what I want.
I looked at the other girls.
Some looked a bit too old but no matter.
Some were incredibly pretty and natural and some were overdressed and over-ready, perfumed, with coiffures, one of them had deep blue eye shadow as if to hypnotize.
She'll do well.
The longer I waited the more concerned I became.
I had come straight from work and I was starting to feel tired.
Waiting.
I was thinking that it's only Wednesday and I had to get through to the

end of the week.
And I also felt unprofessional and ridiculous.
What was I doing there at close to seven in the evening outside a stranger's door?
I felt small in my suit.
The girls who went in seemed to spend a great deal of time in there.
They were retelling their life stories in great detail.

"Yes, of course,"
one of them would say,
"I've had private English lessons from Mr X."
And the girl with the eye shadow would smile for the first time, her smile timed to perfection, showing her pearly whites.

I was definitely tired, leaning against the wall and hoping it would embrace me and protect me from the uncertainty in my mind.
On the phone, she had the voice of a strong woman.
She had a to-the-point voice, someone who knew what she wanted and how to get it.
From what I knew, the agency was run by a husband and wife, the wife with considerable experience, and it sounded like she was in charge of communications.
She got things moving.
And when she opened the door to call me in I immediately saw that she looked the same way she talked.
She had curly hair, from a perm no doubt, and a light shirt with a jacket on top which made her appear professional.
But as I walked inside, and she shut the door behind me, I was not really taken aback by the place.
I had expected something a bit, well, richer!
I hadn't expected an everyday place, with pictures of boats in the corridor and a shoe-rack!
And her husband, or the man waiting in the living room, sitting at a small table, had no smile for me.

"Take your shoes off, Darina, and sit down," she said, right behind me, slightly abrupt and I was starting to worry.

The Wooden Tongue Speaks

I slipped them off and sat in front of him while she came up in front and sat down opposite.
He started it all off.

"I'm going to ask you a few questions in English. They will ask you something similar at the Embassy."

The Embassy was this frightening place and the officers in there would mercilessly question me, trying to find out if I was worthy of entering their country, working there and taking care of their children.

"That's fine,"
I said, feeling anxious about my standard of English, although I had practiced at home.

"Why do you want to work with children?"
It took a minute for my mind to adjust to the sound of English coming from his mouth.

"I love children. You can learn so much from them. Their behavior. I have also learnt a lot about them at university."

"Good. Good."
His English was probably limited to the questions or saying *yes*, *no* or *good*.

"What experience have you got?

"I have worked in voluntary organizations looking after disabled or disadvantaged children."
I had rehearsed this line and I was very happy to use it.

"Good."

"What guarantee do we have that you will come back?"

"I want to come back and start a Masters and learning English will help me do that. I also have no family there," and a Romanian without family is like a fish without water.

"Are you planning to get married there?"

I started laughing in a stupid, almost uncontrolled manner. "No!" He raised his eyebrows as if telling me 'Don't do that at the Embassy.'

"Are you going there for money?"

"No."
This was probably the most ridiculous question. Everybody goes abroad for money and everybody knows.

"Good," and again he had no smile for me, nothing to tell me whether I'd done well or whether I had failed completely.

"Now, what do you know about working as an au pair?"

"You help out the family with their children."

"Yes, but it's an easy job. Very easy. All you do is help out the mother, like you do at home I hope, you do a bit of cooking and cleaning and guess how long you work for?"

"Hmm?"

"About twenty-five hours a week! Can you believe that? Where would you find such an easy job here?"

"I'm more set on America—"

"America! Look, America is overrated. You don't want to go there. The English pound is twice as powerful as the dollar. They have no holidays there and work like slaves. Be smart. Go to England."

The Wooden Tongue Speaks

"I don't know…two friends of mine went to America and, from what I've heard, they're doing very well there."
They've moved on from being au pairs to working in their domains.
In fact they're doing so well they haven't bothered to come back home.

"You need to be smart. Think. The pound is twice as powerful. Twice! Look it up in the exchange rates."
The man didn't even bother to sound enthusiastic.
He'd probably said the same thing a hundred times already.
A thousand times.

"And in England if you work more you get more. Look…" and she bent over and as well as showing me half her tits she also showed me a gold chain.

"You see this chain?"

"Yes."

"This eighteen carat gold chain was given to me as a present when I worked as an au pair in England."

"Really?"

"Have a look at it. Eighteen carat gold. Beautiful!"
She let me touch it and although it looked like any other gold chain seeing her smiley face somehow made it special.

"That's very nice," I said, smiling in response to it all.

"This is a great opportunity for you," said her rather bored husband.

"You will never have an opportunity like this."

"Yes."

Bogdan Tiganov

"You don't know when the next opportunity will be."

"I know. That's why I'm here."

"Right, and let me tell you, you won't find an easier, better paid job than this one. We guarantee you three hundred English pounds a week!
How does that sound?
Fantastic, no?
And you've never been to England but to me it was a wonderful experience.
Everything's clockwork there.
Everybody's polite, helpful, decent and people always have so much in the house you'll never go hungry.
Do you understand me?
You can't because you've never seen anything like it.
A fridge, ceiling high, bursting full of anything you've ever dreamt of.
You like ice cream?
They've got every type imaginable and any time you want something you just go and help yourself.
You don't even have to ask them.
Their home will be your home.
And they take you on holiday with them.
I went everywhere.
Greece, Italy, New York.
You will be like them and they will treat you like a member of their family.
You probably won't even miss your family will you?"
she asked, that near-psychotic grin on her face.

"No, I probably won't."

"And, if you want more money, I mean how much money are you looking to earn anyway, you can easily put an advert in a local shop window and get easy babysitter or cleaning jobs in the evening.
So easy you won't believe they're actually paying you, what ten, twelve pounds an hour for it.
All you do is watch the child and make sure they don't do anything

stupid. That's it.
Or clean the kitchen table, like you do at home.
That's it."
I see her now, how she must've been licking her lips.

"You said you want to learn English.
You can learn English there for free," said the man.

"Your family will tell you what to do. You go to the nearest college and sign up. They're very welcoming."
She was completing his words.
His words and hers were automated responses.
A persuasive jazz.

"You'll love England. It's perfect for you."
I didn't believe the man.
Not at all, but all this while I was thinking no matter what the truth is, no matter what happens, I need to do it, I need a proper paid job, I want to come back and buy a house, I need to learn English, it has to be done.
I'd sold my car already.

"What if I don't like it? What if something goes wrong?"
Oh, what if?
What if the world will end?

"Nothing can go wrong. Your English family have strong links with the agency in England. We are only a small representative branch. As you know, the large agency is based in London. You will have their phone number and address. If things don't go to plan, touch wood, phone them and they'll give you another family straight away."
Where are they?
Where are you?

"Darina, don't think too much. Go for it. You can't lose. You will never have a chance like this one."

"I know. Yes, I know."

Bogdan Tiganov

And I did know.
But I also knew that I was thirsty and sweaty and couldn't make my thoughts connect.

"Have a look," he said, pushing a paper in my direction.
The paper had on it pretty much the same stuff they had told me.
The opportunities.
The reassurance that I wouldn't be stuck with my family forever.

"Read it and sign. We've got a lot more to see today."
The lot were outside their door, waiting to sign like I had been.
I turned the paper over.
There was the usual on there, name, address, references, but apparently I was to sign for fifty pounds a week!
I pointed this out to them.

"That's for the Embassy. If they knew you were going for three hundred they wouldn't let you go."

"Don't worry so much."
How could I not worry?

"Ok, I get it."
Using the pen that was conveniently placed near me, I began filling out the form.

"By the way,"
she said while I was bent over tying my shoelaces,
"it's a good idea to buy your family traditional presents.
They love hand-made traditional stuff.
Dolls.
Embroidery.
Anything traditional.
Maybe even musical…you know?"

"Oh, yeah,"

The Wooden Tongue Speaks

I said, almost stumbling over, hot and realizing that I'd given everything
and had signed away my future.
I had also given them half my money, what I'd worked for, what my brand
new car had been worth.
I only had enough money for a plane ticket back.
And I couldn't really see anything as I left, not even the girl who was
putting on fresh lipstick as I walked towards the stairs.

The Killer

There are many friends in the world and, like everything, friendship is a mystery.
People rely on their friends, bully their friends, humiliate them, love them more than family.
Friends are made from nothing.
Friends are broken and disappear back to nothing.
Everything is strange.
Everything natural can be completely unnatural.
Take the lives, and deaths, of three friends born in a small town lying in south-eastern Romania.
They grew up together like brothers.
Two boys, Daniel and Gheorghe.
One girl, Stela.
Poor children.
Their parents were friends so they, in turn, became friends.
The same future destined to all nobodies.
They played on swings.
They played football.
They sprayed themselves with hosepipes.
They chased dogs.
They got bitten.
They hit each other.
They watched how things moved and grew and stayed still and they got agitated.
They shared problems and they shared sweets.
They swapped boyfriends and girlfriends and they kissed and touched and tried.

The Wooden Tongue Speaks

They decided and they dreamt.
There were far more dreams than results.
They listened to music.
They clapped their hands until sore.
They hated and hated the system.
They learnt.
They cheated.
They helped and ignored each other.
People react more or less the same way to poverty.
They want to get out.
It's only the well-off who prefer to believe that poor people are content.
In this society it is common knowledge that the well-off are scum.
The reason is that everybody's equal here.
Everybody loves the flag.
Everybody loves the leaders, singing the songs that oil the mechanism of the heart.
Daniel was angry about the way things were.
Stela was sad.
Gheorghe didn't care.
Daniel kept telling them.
He kept on it like he was friends with truth.

"Shut up! Please shut up!"

"I don't want to get in trouble."

"You're in trouble already, fool! God! Look what we do to survive!"

"What our parents do actually..."

These arguments were hopeless frustrations.
But in a way they felt like a special group because of their heartfelt beliefs.
A good friendship is when you have a pillar, or several pillars, behind you.
Daniel moved away to university, Stela moved away to a different university and Gheorghe stayed home doing menial jobs at the steel factory.

Bogdan Tiganov

University used to be a special place.
It used to be especially difficult to get into, needing almost perfect grades and superhuman determination.
The professors considered that Daniel had a natural aptitude for art and, more precisely, photography.
His photos had real subtle emotion.
They said he had a God-given talent for capturing the right moment.
A smile, for example, has many a phase.
Daniel captured the phase in which you meant love.
People would honestly stare at his photos and say "I never knew I could look like that."
He made peasants look noble through their apparent pride.
He was also good at painting still life.
For man and woman the central and most important part of life was their food.
You need edible meat that is not fifty percent fat,
red fruity tomatoes,
onion,
peppers,
potatoes,
beans and cabbage,
but not necessarily all on one plate.
And God damn it if food is so important then he thought he would make it look that way on canvas.
You can build a skyscraper, you can go to the moon, but if you don't appreciate good food and a glass of wine you don't know what life is.
Stela went for the safe option.
She went for the option that would make a parent proud.
Medicine.
She got in with average grades of 9.97, which, although sounding impressive, wasn't the highest on the list.
Her problem was she hated blood.
She would forever swallow back disgust in the operating theatre.
But she found fellow doctors to be wilder than any people she'd met or known of before.
Here were doctors drinking, smoking, partying and chatting up girl after girl.

The Wooden Tongue Speaks

She had a great time in the first year and one day, towards the end of that year, a man, who could be said to have looked like a gangster, visited her.
He was close to six foot six, wide, dressed in a black suit.
That's what she noticed first.
His suit.
Then she noticed his eyes.
Iron.
Then she noticed he was speaking to her.
Then she noticed that her friends had left, that she was alone.
He said:
"Sign this."
And she certainly did.
Meanwhile, Gheorghe was growing into a fine looking man.
He loved to grease back his black hair.
On Sundays he prayed.
On Sundays he also went to friends' houses.
There he tasted his first wine.
He loved it.
Work was good.
It made him feel like a man, carrying heavy steel on his back.
His pay was very low but his family supported him.
They knew his pay would eventually get better.
He met a girl at work.
She seemed a bit simple but her simplicity was so cutting and honest it gave him the energy to keep going.
They got married.
He was twenty and she was sixteen.
He got very drunk that night and danced with the Gypsies.
They played and played the accordion,
the dogs ran in circles,
the violins came,
high pitch,
laughter,
drink and jokes and it went like this…
they made love at four o'clock in the morning.
He said he would think about signing the document.
The agent couldn't help but smile.

Bogdan Tiganov

Through these intense fast-moving years the three friends kept in touch by phone.
All their conversations have been deleted from records.
When Stela graduated she had a job waiting for her.
It was a village job and most doctors had a village job at the beginning to get them bruised and ready.
The duties of a village doctor involved getting up at five in the morning and dealing with the mass of people crowded outside the door.
They all spoke at once.
Then you deliver the baby.
Then you tend to colds and infections and you deal out all the antibiotics.
When you run out of medication there is nothing you can do and you have to accept that.
But Stela kept her sense of humor.
And her sense of humanity.
She didn't get down or depressed because the peasants were so beautiful in their naivety and their innocence.

"We're like the water pouring down."

It was one of those days.
Nothing to do but wait for the rain to stop.
She would have to help with repairs but she was trying not to think about that.
An old woman had cooked a meal for her.

"How?"

"We burst from gray, we rush down, we spread, we soak the earth then we disappear."

Sundays she spent at home.
She met with old friends.
They shared a couple of beers.
They were tired and there didn't seem that much to talk about.

When things changed people bought more electronics, videos and

The Wooden Tongue Speaks

cameras.
They began taking snapshots.
Rubbish.
Smiley nothings.
The change was towards a wild superficiality.
Work was harder to come by.
Work was no longer guaranteed.
We can take our own pictures now.
So Daniel was forced to search for other, totally unrelated, work.
He worked, for example, in a supermarket.
People were amazed at cereal and American style chips.
He grew a beard.
He married one of his clients from past times then realized he'd made a mistake.
He then worked in an electronics shop.
He was a man in his late thirties while his co-workers were teenagers so they didn't get on.
They had different attitudes.
Their minds were reeling from unexpected democracy.
His mind was more suspicious.
He ended up slapping one of them and found himself jobless,
at home with the walls and a bottle of țuică[18],
found himself with an unsatisfied flirty woman who called herself his wife
and who was constantly telling him what a let-down he was.
No matter, there is nothing that a blackout can't cure.
He hit her and she left.
He shaved and wormed his way into a job selling mobile phone top-ups
and batteries to hungry consumers.
She came back, their relationship improved but he would never take a photograph again.

It became Stela's priority to search for desolate houses.
When she found one she bought it and renovated it.
She put in leather sofas and marble flooring.
She put in a desk.
It took a few years to buy the expensive equipment but eventually her

---

18 Țuică *is the Romanian national liquor, a plum brandy well known for its potency.*

private cabinet was ready and open to the public.
She married a fellow doctor from the hospital where they worked.
He was very quiet, well-mannered and liked classical music.
In time she discovered that his quietness meant he thought himself superior to everybody else, especially to her.
He said that she was the type to make stupid jokes of tragedies, the type who doesn't take anything seriously, blind to the universal importance of Bach or Chopin.
He began to lecture her and she got quieter.
She changed her approach.
She stopped joking.
She found humor in nothing.
Everything was sad.
Everything was a disaster and heartbreaking.
The future was to be carefully planned out.
Serious success was her aim.
She got pregnant, an even better opportunity for him to patronize her.

"You can't go to work now can you?"

"Yes I can."

"No. You can't. Look at you. You're sick."

"I can work."

And she dragged herself to work, vomiting when she could, her thoughts being a swirl of hate and disgust, but talking her way through and refusing to listen to so-called well-wishers.
She couldn't think and she didn't realize how much this was affecting her.
She hoped her baby was in a good state.
Maybe this was God's way of paying her back for all the people she'd written reports on, all the people who'd been interrogated, humiliated and beaten because of her.
The baby was born and he was healthy with spiky black hair.
Word of mouth had its effect and people came to their private clinic.
The tips were great.

The Wooden Tongue Speaks

They had to be.

Sometimes you find yourself in the position of boss and you don't know what kind of mask to wear because everyone's expecting you to put on the boss mask.
Power hadn't fascinated Gheorghe.
He'd never signed that piece of paper, hence the limp.
But he still found himself boss.
The most well-liked boss since, well since anyone could remember.
And he handed out the salaries when he could even when his own head was on the line.
And he handed out bottles of drink to night workers who were in desperate need of stimulation.
And he let people smoke whenever and wherever they pleased.
And he turned a blind eye to the occasional nap.
And then he got fired.
And then everyone lost their jobs.
The plant got closed down.
The metal was sold off to Turks.
The elderly workers retired.
They found a couple frozen stiff in their studio flat.
Gheorghe became a taxi driver.
It wasn't easy.
He hated driving.
He hated speed.
He hated small spaces.
But his wife didn't care.
For her, being the boss of the largest factory in town and being a taxi driver amounts to the same thing.
A job.
For money.
But he couldn't help comparing past to present.
His job had been more of a home than his actual home.
It was where he'd belonged.
He'd worked there for twenty-five years.
You can't just pick something else up and forget what had slowly injected itself into your blood.

Bogdan Tiganov

Only he was a man with brains.
He was a man who understood that freedom is a fairytale word.
So he got in the damn car and tried to do what was expected.

★

"You know…you know me…you know the way I am…"

"Yes. I know how you are."

"You don't. How long have you known me?"
"Oh…over thirty years?"

"Close to forty."

"Yes."

"And you don't know."

"What don't I know?"

"Never mind."
She looked at him.
He looked old.
He was going bald.
Everything about him was tragic.
Daniel looked back.
He couldn't hold back much longer.

"Tell me…tell me how you can take an old person's last coin so you can
have Italian tiles in your home. To put on a show!"
Now, Stela would normally just walk out on something like this.
But she didn't.
This time she sat and listened.

"How can you take a dying person's last coin so you can buy another villa
in the mountains?"

The Wooden Tongue Speaks

"How can you do that?"

"How can you take a crippled child's coin to buy the latest toy for your child?"

"Can you answer these questions?
Honestly?
Truthfully?
Can you answer them like a human being?
Can you answer them like a friend?"

"How can you take a poor man's chicken or fish and then feed your family with it when you could easily do without it?"

"Why can't you say no?
Why can't you refuse what is not yours?
Why can't you just simply do your job?
Why must you think of yourself above all else?"

He drank his beer in two gulps.
There was more anger now than when he had been a young man.
And the anger was directed straight at his friend.
Like a gunshot.

"Won't you say anything?
Will you just sit there mute because you don't have the guts to face up to what you do every day of your miserable life?
You're not on trial now.
This is not like the movies.
The bad guys don't stand trial here."

Stela hadn't touched her beer.
She called out for another beer for Daniel.
Then she looked directly into his eyes.

"Do you know how much I've loved you?

Bogdan Tiganov

Do you know how much I looked up to you when we were young and you were outspoken about everything?
Do you know how much I admired you for studying what you wanted to not what everybody else wanted?
How much do you actually know?
You think you know about right and wrong.
You think you've done right and I've done wrong.
You think you're some kind of Jesus-like figure while I'm just another society slut.
Well, I'm a doctor.
I've seen people die right in front of me because the government wasn't feeding them, because the government was only feeding the cities and towns.
I've seen malnourished babies crying day and night and their mamas looking like they would prefer to blow their brains out.
And what did anyone do?
Nothing.
We sat there in silent protest.
We told on each other and we made do with what we could get hold of and when we had our taste of freedom we leapt at it like crazed rapists.
We wanted to fuck everyone over and why did we want to do that?
You know, of course you know.
Because you didn't do what most did.
Because you like to think of yourself as an artist.
You didn't mind starving.
But, Daniel, I didn't want to starve.
I wanted to get my own back.
On everyone.
I wanted to shut my family up and I wanted to show you what I could do.
I wanted to reach the top.
And I had the killer instinct to do it whereas you were chickenshit.
If you had any balls you would've done something with your protest rather than keep it personal.
You're no Lenin, though.
You're no Gandhi.
You're a failed, bitter, artist.
Does that explain it?

The Wooden Tongue Speaks

Do you understand how things stand?"

That night Daniel kissed his wife goodnight and went to the kitchen to have a drink.
She got up and told him to come to bed.
He said he would stay another few minutes.
He had another drink.
Then, after she went back to bed in a bad mood, he swallowed all the paracetamol he could find, slit his wrists and, to make sure there would be no way back, slit his neck wide open too.
Stela found out at seven o'clock the following morning.
At first she didn't react.
Then, at lunch, she drove out of town, stopped her car, had a look at the wheat, and stepped in front of a lorry.
"There was something wrong with them."

"They had their problems..."

"Don't we all?"

"They had mental problems too…"

"Probably…"

"Baby?"

"Yes?"

"Let's be careful."

And they were careful to keep themselves happy.
Gheorghe worked as a taxi driver for five years and his wife worked in a furniture store.
They went on holiday twice a year, usually up north to get clean air in their lungs and brains.
Then it was about a week to go till Gheorghe's fiftieth birthday.
They were planning a family get-together.

Bogdan Tiganov

She received a phone call at eleven in the morning.
"Mrs Niculescu?"

"Speaking."

"Your husband had a heart attack."
She noticed the snow.
She noticed…

"Mrs Niculescu? Your husband died on the spot."

She noticed how the snow had covered everything, the gardens, cars, fences and trees.
She noticed it all as the person on the other end told her to come and identify the body.

Jesus, Where Has Everything Gone?

"Do you think Jesus was black? I mean Christ!"

"I don't know, Gabriel. How should I know?"

"Do you think we're worshiping a black man? What would your grandmother say about that? She'd be jumping in her grave, she'd get out in no time, she'd say 'I'm not staying in there if Jesus is black.'"

"Grandmother would come back and die again of a stroke if she heard that Jesus is black."

"That's right. She would."

"Yeah."

They were two old boys with nothing to do.

"Jesus was white, or maybe brown."

"It's a sin to be talking like this."

"Sins? It's a monumental sin what they're doing to this country!"

"They should all be shot."

"No. Dying's too easy. Torture them, very slowly."

"I wouldn't want them taking one more gram of our oxygen."

"Yeah. So torture them, very slowly, then shoot them."

Gabriel had been an engineer, but the plant got closed down so he retired earlier than normal.
The plant got closed down because all the money had gone.

"Even Jesus would have a hard time forgiving these bastards."

"He wouldn't forgive them. He'd let them burn in eternal hell. He'd fry their hearts on the bonfire."

An old woman appeared carrying her shopping.

"Oh, hello Maria."

"Hello Gabriel. How's Izabel? Last time we talked she said her back was hurting her."

"I think she's better now."
She wasn't.
She was worse.

"That's good. Take care, Gabriel, and take care of her."
He wasn't.

"I will. Don't worry."

"Send my love to Carmen."
She was his daughter.
Carmen was a journalist working too much, headaches battered her, her husband an alcoholic doctor.

"I will."

They watched her open the door and turn away.

"That Maria, she sticks her nose in too much."

The Wooden Tongue Speaks

"She's alright. She's senile."

"She's not. She's a cow. You know how she tortured Alex with her constant need for change, always wanting something new, a fur coat, a new fridge, more plants…"

"She's alright."

"I don't think so, Gabriel."

Bela was not well liked.
He kept himself very much to himself.
He adored his privacy.
People didn't know much about him, so they disliked him.
Bela had worked as a driver, lorry driver, taxi driver, bus driver.
He loved to travel, short distances and long.
He loved to move on, to get out.

"I haven't told anybody yet but Carmen's pregnant again."
He'd told plenty of people.

"Congratulations. A grandfather, twice over."

"I don't want her to be pregnant.
She's not a childbearing factory for that piece of shit!"
That piece of shit was Victor, the alcoholic doctor, who was actually one of the nicest guys in town.

"I can't understand that."

"Every time I see him, every time, you know what I want to do?"

"What?"

"Spit in his face."

Bogdan Tiganov

"I'm sure she knows what she's doing."

"She doesn't know anything. She's inherited her mother's pigheadedness."

"Carmen will learn her lesson."

"But I don't want it to be too late.
I don't want her to end up a mess."

"Don't worry, she's a grown woman.
What is she, thirty-four?"

"Thirty-five this year."

"Then don't worry."

They sat on a bench outside the flats.
It was morning, and the neighbors whipped their rugs on the balcony.
The stray dogs had been awake for a long time.
Earlier, the sky had punished them with rain.
Lots of it.

"I need to go."
Where was he going?
He always needed to go, a single man like that…

"Look at the garden."

"It's a disaster, I know."

"They just don't care any more.
They don't care about anything.
They're like wild beasts."

"You're right. They're animals."

The Wooden Tongue Speaks

"There's no control any more. This democracy. Freedom."
He paused to deliver his conclusion. "It's a mistake."

"I know…but I need to go."

"Fine."
"Take care."

They shook hands.
Gabriel was left on his own.
He felt himself shaking.
It was the high blood pressure.
It was the smoking.
It was the bad news.
He got up.
He went past the children's park,
now unusable due to overgrown weeds,
and he walked past the next block where he had to be very careful not be
seen by the mean dog that waited patiently to bite naive walkers.
Generally he liked dogs, even stray ones.
He would bring them leftovers near the dump.
But this dog was too mean.
Rabid.
The land used to be different.
It used to be well kept.
There were rules and you had to follow them.
The land used to be rich.
The land used to be important.
Now it's a dump.
And again he replayed, in his mind, the fantastical scene in which all
politicians are round up, driven to a large hall and shot.
His eyes were practically shut, slits of eyes, piercing what he had to see.
The roads were like obstacle courses.
You couldn't drive on those roads.
The paint was peeling,
the brick was decomposing,
the antennas were crooked,

Bogdan Tiganov

one big earthquake and the whole town would collapse.
He said hello to a few people, then walked on appalled by what he saw.
It was a bomb site.
A war zone.
How could there be a little girl going for a walk with her grandfather?

"Good morning Gabriel."
"Good morning Adi."

"How are you?"

"Fine, and how is Aurelia?"
The little girl was very shy.

"Come on Aurelia, talk to uncle Gabriel, it's uncle Gabriel!"

The little girl didn't want to know about uncle Gabriel because uncle Gabriel looked like a scary old man with small eyes and a big nose.
"She's a good girl."

"She certainly is.
Very talented.
You know she makes up her own poems?
Can you believe that?
Come on, Aurelia, tell uncle Gabriel one of your poems."

The little girl tried to hide behind her grandfather but then she reappeared with her head tilted slightly upwards.

"The little dog
Fell on the log,
He said to me
He found a tree.

He wagged his tail
Got out on bail,
He said to mummy

The Wooden Tongue Speaks

He want the tummy.

He got sweet kisses
Then reminisces
And came to you
In one big shoe."

When she finished she looked shy again.
"Bravo! That's fantastic!"

"She's a genius. Seven years old, can you believe that?"

"It's amazing. I love children."
He didn't.
He had been horrified when confronted with his daughter growing up, not understanding what she wanted, what she needed, her mood swings and curiosity.

"Why don't you come round for dinner tonight?"

"Maybe, maybe…I'll tell Izabel about it and let you know."
He planned to watch football.

"I hope you come. I've got some good wine and managed to get hold of those olives you like."

"Sounds great. I'll let you know in the afternoon."

"Good, Gabriel, don't get too sad about things."

"What do you mean?"

"Try to relax."

"I am relaxed."

"Good. Alright, I'll talk to you later."

Bogdan Tiganov

"See you."

"Bye."

And he waved to little Aurelia, the girl with the large green eyes who could make up poems.
The little girl, what would she know?
So full of snow, she needs to grow!
He was pleased with that.
He could rhyme too.
But now he was tired, so tired so quickly.
And they were gone, turned the corner.
There was no bench to sit on.
There was only the gray dusty road,
the fences,
the weeds and shattered glass,
and the rectangular blocks,
four or five levels,
the old cars with the flat tires and coughing engines.
There was no bench to sit on.
There were only the crows perched on high places and swooping from above to land disappointed in the dust where nothing grows and nothing will ever grow again.
There was only that,
and only the timid sparrows that have lost their colors and their stomachs, small-feathered dots overpowered by a lack of green.
There was no bench as the benches were usually hacked into pieces and sold.
Simply and shockingly the dreary sky no one saw no one cared about which dealt people enough misery with too much or too little rain,
or when the sun came it burnt everything,
made everything redder,
melted the clothes to your skin.
There was no bench to sit on and he felt sick,
he felt like he would vomit or fall over.

The Wooden Tongue Speaks

But instead he lit another cigarette and forced himself to focus again.
He didn't like to walk.
The thoughts would not die down,
the thoughts would not go away,
the thoughts would not leave him alone,
the thoughts would not give him time to breathe.
He smoked his cigarette and made his way home.
Gabriel had strong legs.
It was from years of heavy lifting.
But that day the stairs looked steeper than usual.
They seemed wider, higher, sharper.
He waited a few minutes.

When he got in he smelt the cooking.
Izabel, like normal, was in the kitchen.
Lunch was on the way.
He asked her how she was feeling.

"Alive."

Then he went to her, slowly.

"What is it?"

He gave her a full kiss on the lips.

⭐
The Heart of a Woman

Luiza likes the company of Irina.
She likes her company mainly because she can feel superior and in charge.
She can feel like a mother or sister figure.
Irina weeps every time they meet, which is every other day.
Adrian, Cosmin, Răzvan, Anton, they are all causing her to feel unhappy.
Luiza keeps telling her to get out, to leave, to be independent.
She encourages Irina to be strong.
But the more Luiza tells her to be strong the weaker Irina feels.
And so goes the endlessly repeating cycle.

"What's wrong with that woman? She looks like she's about to disappear."

"She's got no character.
They treat her like a slave and she just takes it.
I mean the other day I was round there and Adrian was sitting a foot away from the ashtray and he asks Irina, who is in the kitchen, to come and hand him the ashtray!
Can you believe that?
Can you imagine if you asked me to do that?"

"Yes, you'd beat my head against the wall."

Florin would like his wife to be a little less manly.
She is too mouthy.
He has to say everything she cooks is unbelievably tasty otherwise she

The Wooden Tongue Speaks

refuses to cook.
He has to compliment her all the time on how she looks or on how wonderfully well she cleans otherwise she asks him if he loves her and if he doesn't love her then what the hell is he doing living with her? Therefore, he can't completely love her. Sure she always looks and smells impeccably but she is too much like his boss.
"Anyway, time will sort her out."

"What do you mean by that?"

"I mean if she just accepts the role of doormat then she's going to pay the price in the long-term."

"It's easy for you to say, though, isn't it? You wouldn't ever have to be in that position. Mama for example…"
but he's heard the story plenty of times of her heroic mother, who'd taken all the shit in the world from her husband and outlived him.

"I know, darling, but times change and she's got to keep up with the world."

"You go and help her if you're so worried about her."

"You're her friend. Go over there and make her divorce that idiot."

"Don't be stupid.
I should divorce you considering how you seem to spend as much time as possible at work and as little time as possible with me."

"Don't joke like that. It's not funny."

"Then don't talk about divorce.
Mama didn't divorce tata so why should I talk other people into divorcing? It's too easy to divorce and much more difficult to work things out."

At this point he would like to have said "Don't use your mama as an example for everything" but he didn't say that because he knew that she would drive a knife down his throat.

"Ok, forget about divorce. She should tell him how things are, how she feels, how she wants to be treated."

"She can't do that!
She can't even raise her voice at him without starting to tremble!
He terrifies her.
I don't know how many times he's beaten her.
Broken arms.
Battered face.
You can't talk to someone as violent and as crazy as that.
The police don't care…"

"Then what should she do?
She can't leave him, she can't fight him, she can't tell him how she feels, what else is there?"

"She's got to make him realize her worth.
Take the kids and go somewhere for a few weeks and he'll realize exactly how much she does for him and how much he depends on her.
Watch how he goes down on his knees and begs for forgiveness."

"But the kids, the kids, baby, they aren't much better than their father. Have you heard how they order Irina to sleep on the floor? Their father's told them that it's better for mama to sleep on the floor so she knows her place and because they're boys they think they have a God-given right to treat their mama like a slave. I wouldn't be surprised if they make her do their homework!"

This talk of kids isn't going down well.
Luiza is desperate to have kids but Florin doesn't want any.
He says he is too young for children.
Children make you feel old.
He is frightened and, every time they have sex, hopes the condoms work their magic.

The Wooden Tongue Speaks

"Those kids need a mother not a wet rag!
Don't you think they need their mama to put her foot down and show them what she can do?"

"I suppose so…"

★

She has to be perfect with her cooking.
A little too much salt or not enough onions and he'd tell her to go and feed the dogs with it.
He comes in the kitchen to smoke and she pretends not to mind that he is analyzing her cooking.

"Looks ready to me."

"A few more minutes."

"Do you want me to starve to death?
Do you know how hard I've worked today?
Do you know how tired I am of incompetence?"
She makes a move to wipe something but it goes on the floor.

"It's nearly ready. Don't worry. I'm nearly-"
only he grabs her by the neck and pulls her up off her feet.

"Listen to me you ungrateful bitch.
I want my food ready when I come back from work not two hours later!
How would you like it if I brought the pay home two months late?
You wouldn't, would you?
Now put that shit on a plate and let me have it!"
and he drops her back on her feet gasping for air.

Adrian feels like slapping the small, pathetic looking woman in front of him. One hard slap to teach her one important lesson.
His arm's telling him that it is ready to swing.

Bogdan Tiganov

"Listen to me you fucking cunt!
Have you been drinking my wine?
Have you had yourself a lovely little party?
You and your whore friends?
Listen to me!"
and he runs after her through the narrow corridor.
She shuts the door in his face.

"Help! He's trying to kill me! Help!"
She's shouted these words many times and only once have the police come, talked to them for a few minutes and left looking amused with the whole situation.
He barges open the door and she is on the floor having fallen over the bed.
Terrified.

"Don't I give you enough?
Do you want my fucking soul as well?
Do you want me to crawl on the floor like a retard and beg for your titty?
Do you?
Is that what you want?
You slimy whore!
You and your fucking family!"
When he said that his foot slammed her head.
The follow-up kick is harder.

The three boys are in their room.
Cosmin is too small to understand anything.
He just feels the fear and agony in his bones moving through him and then like one sharp arrow straight through his heart.
Răzvan is afraid his tata might come and beat them as well.
He is sure his tata has plenty of reasons to beat them.
Like he didn't get a perfect ten for math.
And Anton is proud of his tata.
He is a real man.
You don't see real men like his tata on the street.
His tata walks tall.

The Wooden Tongue Speaks

Alone.
In control of his life.

It's always been the heart of a woman that has saved what was there to be saved.
Through the many, many years.
In the nights when you could've easily have used the kitchen knife to end it.
When you doubted yourself.
Always the heart of a woman.
Irina tells herself these words when she is in physical and mental pain.
She tells herself these words to make herself get up in the morning and face the working day.
Sometimes she surprises herself, when she's walking to the bus stop in the morning, finding that she's said the words out loud.
Tonight, though, she has forgotten the words and her head's ringing instead.
One resonant gong.

★

"I can't seem to find your pension…"

"It should be here today. I was told it would be here today."

"I know, madam. Let me have another look."

She turns to look but she can't see the drawers well.
She reaches up with her right hand to place her spectacles higher up her nose so she can see better but the spectacles are already there.
Irina shakes her head at her own stupidity.
Sighs and collapses.

"Darling! There's no need for that!"

"Oh, leave me alone…"

Bogdan Tiganov

When she presses the buzzard she knows her face is red and her hands are shaking.
She tells herself to keep her voice steady.
He looks through the eyehole.
He knows why she is here.
Irina's other friends have already phoned to bitch and moan at him.
The kids are staying with their interfering grandparents.
Adrian opens the door expecting a hurricane.
"What do you want?"

"I want you to admit that you're an arrogant, wife-beating, coward!"

"No need to shout. Come in. The neighbors know too much already."
He is half drunk and feels like slapping this cow around.
She steps in and he shuts the door.

"Sit down. Would you like a drink?"

"Are you certifiably insane?
Do you think I'd want to hold anything that's been touched by your cowardly hands?"

"Why don't you just call the police like everyone else?"

"Call the police?
The police are more likely to arrest me!"

"Right, and they should arrest you...
what exactly do you want to resolve by shouting at me?"

She wants to beat him to a pulp.
She wants to serve out justice because she thinks she is able to and nobody else can.

"That woman is everything you've got.
Everything that's made you what you are today.
Everything that keeps you alive.

The Wooden Tongue Speaks

Without her you don't exist."

He laughs, "Yeah…right…" and takes a drink.

"That's right.
Without her you're a baby in danger.
You're a crystal dish in the middle of a lion's den.
Think about it.
Think about what you've done and the fact that it's too late to change anything.
That's right.
It's too late for regrets.
It's too late to rethink!
And when she comes out of hospital, after her operation, I will make sure she has nothing more to do with you.
Get me? I'll personally hammer all the nails in your coffin."

He stares at her and says, calmly
"You can't do that. I'll set fire to your house,"
and he takes another drink in an assured manner.

"You don't know what I'm capable of.
If I see you anywhere near my house I'll scratch your fucking eyes out."
Then she practically jumps over to where he's standing, grabs his wineglass and throws it at the television.
The glass breaks.
The television doesn't.

"I wish that television had blown up,"
she says then spits in his face.

"And what did he say?"

"He didn't say anything.
He's a coward and cowards have nothing to say."

Bogdan Tiganov

Florin is trying to watch the news.
It's all about car crashes and suicides.

"You shouldn't've done that.
God knows what he'll do.
He might come and throw a stone through our bedroom window!"

"He won't do that. Cowards don't do that."

★

Luiza goes to get the mail.
She is always checking the letterbox on her way to work.
In the mail there are three envelopes.
Two of them are bills, the other one is brown.
She gets in her car and drives to work, yawning yet quite awake.

"So you're divorcing me. You're showing me what you can do?"

"Something like that…"
His eyes are staring at her feet.

"Good. Let's do it."

★

"I've got my own place now so you can come and stay with me until you
sort something out."
She is looking so much better, brighter in the face.

"No. I can't. I've got a family to go to."
Luiza looks at Irina trying hard to swallow some salad.

"It's always been the heart of a woman that has saved what was there to
be saved don't you think? Am I wrong?"

Luiza doesn't answer.

The Wooden Tongue Speaks

She can't answer.
She has to turn her back.

After the divorce, Luiza found a new man as characterless as the previous. He was intimidated by her and he was quite surprised, but quite delighted, when he found a note one morning on the kitchen table:

"I'm going. There's nothing for me in this place.

I can't stomach the absurdity of it all.

If you like, I can't stomach men.

I can't stomach relationships.

They're making me sick.

So I'm quitting and this is my notice.

I never thought I'd be a quitter but you don't need to worry about that.

I'm sure you'll find another victim to help you along."

Luiza

The Meal

Tiberiu had decided that everyday life was just something you had to accept and go on with.
Things happen, be it happiness, arguments, poverty, and most of the time there's nothing that can be done apart from swallowing hard.
A fine example: every morning he faced up to a job that wasn't paying.
0 and assurances and he was behind on bills, borrowing money having used up his savings long ago.
There was not a chance of sending the kids to university.
Only if over night they turned into geniuses and were awarded foreign grants.
Another example: the chances of this happening was 0 because his kids were not Mozarts or Da Vincis but were, instead, assholes, stealing from his pockets
(if they found a coin or note in the house they assumed it was theirs)
to buy alcohol and cigarettes.
Oh yes, being modern and democratic means doing nothing with your life.
Therefore, the kids had to be forgotten about immediately.
Being a furniture salesman was about as rewarding for the soul as imagining having his tongue bit into by a pit bull.
And he would prefer that to being trapped in a room with colleagues he could not understand.
Many times he found himself wondering whether they were actually speaking the same language.
More recently, however, he had ceased caring and looking to understand.
To hell with them! To hell with this country and this miserable life!
For a salesman, Tiberiu wasn't friendly.
He simply couldn't pretend.

The Wooden Tongue Speaks

He tried to be friendly with the intelligent connoisseur who knew the value of quality, wood, craftsmanship, hand carved rather than machine processed, but towards most, who brushed artifacts with their eyes like hardened criminals would, he had no enthusiasm.
Cretins!
By midday he had had enough of everything and of himself.
He couldn't breathe as his body was suffocating him.
The daylight, which would soon fade to black, was a cruel reminder that out there nature and other free creatures had a reach
far exceeding his own.
The stray dog, for example, the one casually taking a dump outside the window, is free to walk wherever he *(or she)* pleases, do and discover as much of the world as he *(or she)* wants.
And the stray dog is not held back by shackles and manacles and prisons and delusions created by mankind's superior brain.
The luck of the stray dog, not seeing and not appreciating civilization!
Damn the stray!
A customer would walk in, an animal of a man, looking to fill up his villa.
We have this dresser handmade in Florence…and what about these classical chairs? Look at those beautiful, carved legs.
The customer, sporting an unusually large, round head with a short haircut that would look wrong on anyone, would simple stare and then say:
"From Italy? Who, then, handmade it?"
These are the people who can say what they like, can behave
how they feel.
The rest of us choke on our spit.
Tiberiu could not answer.
"I'm only playing! Only joking with you! But listen…call me when you come across anything…worthwhile…" he would say and bounce out the shop as he would bounce out of most shops on Boulevard Dorobanților where Tiberiu worked.
Because the day felt unrelenting when he got home all he wanted to do was smoke.
His insides were complaining and his eyes were wired open due having drunk large mugs of black coffee.

Bogdan Tiganov

And all he wanted to do was smoke and not say a word.
And while he was smoking one of the children, one of the boys, the younger, would come and take his cigarette pack away.
Then his wife would switch on the cooker and the air would become unbearable – boiler-like.
So he would step out on the balcony but when he looked at the gypsies, the groups of young ones and yapping dogs, he didn't see anything as if looking straight through them.
At gaps.
He kept staring until the call for dinner.
Dinnertime was different now.
A limited affair.
Mihaela would be there and sometimes his middle child.
Never the youngest one and never the daughter.
But the food, the food was to be thrown back and forgotten about.
It was what it was.
Beans or fried potatoes or mămăligă and goat's cheese.
It was beans with bits of meat that could pass untouched through the teeth.
If only there was enough to catch onto and dig his teeth into and spend a fair while chewing!
He would ask his son about school and his son would shrug and say very little.
They had forgotten how to speak these young ones.
Or maybe they just didn't want to speak to him.
Maybe they were afraid of him, or of his age, or ashamed of his presence.
So they didn't feel it necessary to exercise their vocal chords.
His son knew everything, of course, and, at the same time, next to nothing.
He could tell you the latest PC specifications but knew nothing of world geography or history.
He had no idea why his parents were like they were.
Not enough ambition!
Not enough risk taking!
Content doing small-time work!
So you lost your job – so what?
Happens to most people, doesn't it?

The Wooden Tongue Speaks

After the meal his son would go to his computer and his wife would find something to do, like rearranging the kitchen so he could not find what he wanted.
Tiberiu would go and watch TV for a few hours.
He watched the news, the weather forecast, a film if it was on, if not then some sort of documentary on Discovery Channel.
Nobody came into the living room.
At half past ten Mihaela would go to sleep because she was that bit stronger and that bit better regimented than he was.
He didn't want to sleep and he didn't want to stay awake either.
He didn't want to be there thinking and he didn't really want to watch TV or turn it off and face it.
He didn't want to listen to the neighbors or wait for his daughter to come home at gone one reeking drunk and desperate to find the toilet.
He didn't need the lights on or off.
He wanted an in-between.
Why was there no in-between?
On the second shelf of the bookcase, near the window, crushing the book next to it, was the Collected Works of Mihai Eminescu[19].
Nobody had read this giant of a book in decades.
He slipped a note in there.
It wasn't much but that's what he could allow for.

★

"You're going to come – and you will stay for lunch and dinner-"
he said while pulling on his sleeve.
His youngest turned to give him that look and twist his arm away.

"Don't know. What's the point?"

"The point is…the point is…"

What is the fucking point, anyway?

Mihaela was not the most confident of cooks so her mama would come

---

19 *Mihai Eminescu (1850-1889) is the National Poet of Romania.*

to help and reassure her.
They sat in the kitchen squeezing pig meat into open bladders, something he found pleasurable as he liked to see the formation of a product.
In fact, he'd love to have studied carpentry so he could create with his hands.
What use were hands if they did nothing but hang limply by his side?
He listened to them talking and they had a lot to talk about, not having seen each other for a good day or so.
His mother in law was an older version of his wife.
The same wicked grin.
The eyes of coal and hellfire.
They also shared a determination he couldn't understand.
They appeared to believe in the words they spoke.
When he wasn't listening he delighted in seeing the meat crushed into shape.
He turned the handle as she talked about her colleagues and the winter holidays they would soon be having.
When are we going on holiday?
When are we flying off to Rome or Paris?
Ahh…Paris.
Never.
He couldn't remember the last holiday they'd had in 85 when they went to Sinaia and skied for the first and only time.
The older version talked about her friends and her brother who was half crazy with dementia and who tried drinking out of the toilet bowl.
Why not? Why not?
And then she asked him about work and how business was going and he said:
"The business is going to shit."
She nodded in response like it was only natural that business would go to shit and then she started a rant on the children, a subject that she excelled at.
Why don't you discipline them?
When tata winced we ducked our heads!
And Mihaela got some fine beatings too…
for spitting on a girl at school,

The Wooden Tongue Speaks

for throwing up her dinner,
for not turning up at the dentist's,
for cheating on her boyfriend with another friend,
reasons that gave life to her personal story and made her feel that her early history had substance and vibrancy while the present was a dying disappointment.
Will they end up on the streets?
How can they work an honest job when they can't be bothered to get up in the morning?
How can they learn when they don't want to study, they don't feel like it, and the teachers are unqualified anyway because all the good ones leave!
Yes and even if they finish university they won't find a job.
Good kids doing all sorts.
Poor kids.
Living in a crazy world.
All this and more she said while also scooping out the marrow core and slicing up carrots and dicing up cucumber…

He woke up earlier than usual.
Slightly agitated.
And, for a moment, sad.
She had awoken already.
Then, he looked in every room and they were empty.
He made sure they were empty before going to the bathroom where he shaved and put on aftershave and then walked round again tidying up what he thought stood out.
When she came back she found him, as usual, at the kitchen table, drinking his coffee, sipping philosophically, smoking his cigarettes.

"How was church?"

"Good."

Mihaela turned round to go and, then, she stepped out and he meant to ask her if she wanted a drink.
Only Tiberiu didn't.

Bogdan Tiganov

They began arriving and he was at the door shaking hands.
Kissing cheeks.
Smooth cheeks.
Perfumed cheeks.
Bearded cheeks.
He helped take off their coats and lay them on the hooks.
He showed them where to leave their shoes and he told them not to worry about the dirt from the mud and snow.
Mihaela led them to the table.
Others would come late, if at all.
His place was near the far end.
Next to him a friend of the family had made himself comfortable and began immediately his commentary.

"You're looking good."

"Ah…"

"You are. You've put on weight."

"From sitting too much. And waiting."

"Sitting eh? I'd like to sit once in a while too but I can't, I can't, my stomach won't let me," he said, laughing.
He worked on his own vinery.
The EU were promising funds but he hadn't smelt the Euros yet.
The promises, though, helped lift his legs and arms and bend his back when necessary.

"I can't even touch the stuff these days."

"Oh yeah?

"It's the liver you know? I don't want any more things popping inside."
He'd had two heart attacks and suffered from bladder problems.

"It's a worry…"

The Wooden Tongue Speaks

"It's a curse.
My father drank all his life.
No problem.
Nothing bothered him."

"How did he die?"

"He's not dead. We just don't talk,"
and he guffawed so loud the cutlery shook,
or maybe that was from his shaky knees bumping the table.

"But I don't need to worry about that today, do I? Do I, baby?"
he asked his wife who tried hard not to hear him.

"Do I darling baby honey?"

"Do you what?" she snapped back.

"You hear the tone of that woman?
You hear how she talks to her loving, highly sensitive husband?"

"Well…"

"Fuck it. Noroc!"
he spat out and poured himself two fingers of vodka then drank it down
like medicine for the soul.

"Noroc," Tiberiu said, following suit and feeling better for it.

"How's life in Bucharest?" he asked his cousin in front.
She worked as a dentist, doing well financially.
She was divorced.
Three times.

"Wonderful! Money grows on trees like it's supposed to."

"Our trees are the same. Only we can't see the cash because of the snow."

"Oh but when that snow melts away…New Year new possibilities…"

"Not as long as I'm alive."

"Hey! You never know!"

"Noroc!"

That's what we're ever dependent on.
Luck.

It went quiet, almost, as Mihaela brought in the sausages and they had first servings of the salată de boeuf[20].
It was reasonably silent until one or two of them starting praising the food.

"I like it," said one of them.

"Has a bit of spice. What is that? Mustard? And this," continued she,
"is perfect."

"Yes," confirmed her husband.

A woman close-by nodded in approval.
On the other side, in the far corner, Tiberiu paused and watched them.
Eating.
Talking.
He saw how they tasted the various kinds of sausages, the home-made and the store bought.
They pinched their bread and sucked on it with the juices helping to cement the taste.
The salad seemed to be especially popular as most were having seconds.
He thought nothing.

---

20 *Romanian salad dish made of diced vegetables and meat with lots of mayonnaise.*

The Wooden Tongue Speaks

Then somebody switched on the music and the tune crackling out of the computer speakers was old, melancholy and romantic.

After the first course he lit up.
His friend had brought a couple of bottles of red wine and he placed these proudly on the table and proceeded to fill up peoples' glasses.

"I told you," he said after their first sip, "not as good as last year's."

But the roast was as good.
It was tastier.
Fuller.
Mihaela had used a special, secret recipe and dripping fat lingered on the tongue while the taste buds shivered.
Maybe, he thought while his heart beat with unbelievable pride, they need more bread to go with this.

The Verdict

You get gut sick.
From the moment everything hits you there's nothing in the world that can save you.
It happens when you think the past is gone and forgotten.
Gut sickness.

"God!"

Suddenly you want God on your side.
You go to church.
You went last in 90.
But it's worse.
The incense, the holy words, these make it far worse.
Surely you can't cry, not you with the big balls and big belly.
No way, not even this horrifying sickness can get to you.
You put a strong wall up a long time ago.
It's one o'clock.
One more minute.
She will come.
Moaning.
Bitching.
This is definitely not what you imagined would happen.
She's changed for the worse.
Power scrunched up her mind.
And she's better than you.
In every way.
She is more.

The Wooden Tongue Speaks

But she looks terrible this late with her hair sticking up and her wrinkles clearly showing in feeble light.
She's looked terrible for years no matter how much make-up she's used.

"What are you doing?"

You can't answer.
Not now.

"Have you lost it? What do you think you're doing sitting there so late drinking ţuică?"

Her voice is an echo far away, possibly in another room lost by the time it gets to you.

"You have to be ready at five. And you can't hold down your alcohol. Don't be stupid…"
She knows exactly how it is.

There is no problem.
You're just feeling a little sad.
Maybe it's the dark skies of winter.
Be careful.
These roads are yours and you know them well.
How well?
Your name in capitals.
Precisely painted in red.
Park right there and walk out proud.
It's early and nobody cares if you stumble.
Night time.
Sleep.
You can't see very well but you know which way to go.
Use your instinct.
You've done this so long, so many hours, six, seven days a week, thirty years.
Retirement's not a bad idea.
Retirement?

Bogdan Tiganov

You feel sick at the thought and much too sick.
You go in to your office, determined.
You lock your door and open the drawer in your desk taking out the bottle of țuică.
You find some old cigarettes and light one.
Everything's swimming.
Gut sickness but you can't vomit.
Nothing comes out.
You need the alcohol.
You rub your face trying to get some blood working.
What is this?
Cancer?
It's not like you to worry.
You're a happy-go-lucky character.
Your smile is heavenly.
People admire you, look up to you.
Only your children don't.
The two boys.
The two alcoholics.
They haven't learned anything.
Use and use and abuse.
Idiots.
Simply one of life's many disappointments.
This is not like you, you, you, who the hell are you?
Sitting in this office like a king.
Your cigarette's finished.
Light up another.
Stretch over and open the window. More țuică.
How dare you?
How dare you cry?
Someone's knocking and you don't panic.
You don't worry.
You can stand and you can walk and you manage to slowly unlock the door.
It's the sister in charge.
She's usually very pleasant.

The Wooden Tongue Speaks

"Hello, Doctor."

"Hello, Ana."

"How are you?"
She can smell your breath.
"Same as usual. And you?"

"Tired. Need more sleep."

"We all need more."

"Like lions."
You try to chuckle.
It comes out rough.
Your spittle clings to her.

"You have seven operations today."

"Is that all?"

"Seven would kill me."
And she walks around the office looking for something.

"I don't know."
Today you feel like one operation will kill you.

"When is the board review?"

"In two weeks."

"Tell them we need more syringes."

"I will."

She has a nasty side.
It comes out when she needs something.

Bogdan Tiganov

The anesthetic can leave you suffering from hallucinations for the rest of your life.
White circles and red circles and elephants sucking in and out in perspective.
They don't tell you that.
They only tell you what is necessary.
It is a dark room, a morgue, a sanctuary.
It is extremely dark where you are standing.
It has never been darker, pulling you down into the earth.
There are no sounds, nothing that is reminiscent of breathing.
Rats.
In a cold cellar.
Morning, night, afternoon.
Your hands are lost in the mist, plunging on instinct.

"What is he doing? That incision is wrong!"

"He knows best."

"Not any more.
Not recently.
He knows about the bottle."

"Shut your mouth before he hears you."

"He's heard me.
I've told him.
He doesn't care.
You can tell him anything and he doesn't care, isn't that RIGHT Doctor?"

"Right."

★

You feel hot.
Your uniform is strangling you.

The Wooden Tongue Speaks

Your desk is a barrier keeping you away from reality.
And yet you're on the other side looking at this fat, trembling, burning wreck.
They're knocking.
They're all knocking.
The whole town wants to see you.
You are theirs.
One hundred percent.
To the last molecule.

"Come in. Come in!"

He comes in,
wearing peasant clothes,
unshaven,
most probably unwashed.
Just look at that.
The times haven't changed anything.
Oh God no.

"I need some medicine, Doctor."

"Sit down."

He sits down.
He's got sad green eyes.
Most of the peasants have these sad green eyes.

"What do you need?"

"Insulin, Doctor."

"Who's got diabetes?"

"My daughter, Doctor.
She's dying."

Bogdan Tiganov

Rewind.
Thirty or so years ago this would've broken your heart.
But you sold off pity, heart and care.
You had to.
99% of people had to.
No choice.
You had to.
There was choice.
There was choice!
As you stare through, past him, you see he left the door open and you see mothers and old women and a child with one eye shut.

"Here, Doctor."
You grab the bag.
What's inside is irrelevant.

"Go two doors right and tell Ana to give you some."

"Thank you."

He tries to smile and so do you and you know there is no insulin left to give.
You can only take, no time for anything as the next peasant enters looking worse than the previous.
It feels ridiculous from where you are because you should be feeling powerful, a mighty man, a man with a valuable reputation.
People stop their cars to talk to you.
People stop what they're doing to ask you what you need and the years have felt extraordinary until last month.
That's when reality pulled its clear mirror out and stuck it to your face.
It's quiet.
He's waiting for you.

"And what do you want?"

"Well, Doctor….I'm supposed to be having my heart operated on this week."

The Wooden Tongue Speaks

"So?"

"I'd really like…to know…what my chances are."
You look through your papers but you can't see.

"Your chances are good."
He doesn't believe you.
He sees through you.

"Your chances are very good.
Don't torment yourself.
Stay off the wine."
Still no answer.

"Listen…do you have a cigarette?"
He takes out his pack and hands you one.

"Close the door."
He gets up, plenty of years older than you, or at least he looks that way
but he could be younger.
The door clicks.
You hear mumbles of disagreement on the other side.

"I want you to answer me honestly."
He nods.

"What do you think my chances are?"
You light your cigarette.
You take out your bottle and offer it.
He takes plenty.

"I don't understand, Doctor."

"I feel like I'm going.
I feel like the end is coming.
I feel like there is no exit to rely on.
Do you understand?"

Bogdan Tiganov

He takes more.
He lights his cigarette.

"I think I understand. And you…you want me to be honest?"

"Yes. Don't worry. Your operation is covered."

"I can't, Doctor. I can't…"

"Please.
I'm begging you.
Tell me the truth.
I know you can do that."

"I can't. I don't know much…"

"I know you don't want to risk anything but look…" and you take a piece of paper that your hand falls on and you write on it that you guarantee him professional treatment no matter what he says and you sign your name on it, stamp it and give it to him.
He looks at it and continues to smoke.
The ash goes on the floor.

"I don't know…"
It feels like you have two heads – one head is moving up, the other dead fruit.
Yet, you feel for your wallet and slide out the notes from in there.
You put it on the desk.

"Just a few honest words and you get this cash."
Someone knocks.

"Wait!"
The knocking stops.
Temporarily.

"Right.

The Wooden Tongue Speaks

Tell me.
Now."
He looks you straight in the eyes.

"Alright, Doctor.
The truth is you don't deserve to live.
You deserve to be flogged, worked to death.
You deserve to be shot.
The diseases and pains in this hospital should affect only you.
The truth is that alcohol you've been using won't help you.
Nothing will help.
God won't help you.
It's much too late for help, Doctor.
You're going to hell soon where the Devil will grind his teeth on your bones."

"Ok."

You take the cash and put it back in your wallet.
You are not red in the face.
You are not nervous.
You are not drunk.

"Now I'll tell you something, my dear little peasant.
Your chances are zero.
And I'll make it my priority to keep your chances at zero."
He's finished his cigarette and his hands are clenched together.

"That's what I thought would happen."
He's up, sweaty, unwashed, gray, overworked.

"Stay true to your instincts."

With his back to you he says "Thank you, Doctor," then the door clicks shut.

"Thank you."

Bogdan Tiganov

You feel much better now.
Ready and content.

Gap

The tiny mirror in the bathroom, my eyes are bloodshot, tired, lost, will never again recover.
And yet here is where I get my peace.
It's not much, is it?
There is no escape from these little boxes where everybody's arguments echo off the walls.
Only a few limited moments and even then your heart races ahead, worried about what will happen, giving you no time.

"Have you fallen down the toilet?"

I laugh.
My sister.
She always wants to use the bathroom.
She needs one to herself.
Really.

"Ok, ok."

I open the door and step out.

Vali's living on another planet.
I mean I love him but sometimes I think I have to.
You wouldn't know he's older.
A little boy.
I don't know what he's doing.
Get ready.

Bogdan Tiganov

The whole class is watching me.
They're waiting for my foreign looks.
Bewitching.
The queen.
I'm interesting.
It's important to stay that way.
I love this red.

★

Today, mama, my day was wrong.
No, I don't want to cry.

"Take it. Accept that we don't belong."
I know.
Don't think that I could possibly forget.

"Touch it with this."
It hurts.
You don't love me.

"Don't be a baby. You're fourteen. Don't be weak."
Weak.
I'm not weak.
I hate the word.
You're not listening.
You're not interested.

"Baby, I care.
Please don't cry.
I'm in your position too.
Every day I wish it were different.
But what can I do? Eh?
Do you want me to go to work crying and working the machinery
while I'm crying?
Do you want me to lose my job?
You know what that would mean…"

The Wooden Tongue Speaks

"I'm sorry."
I'm sorry I was born.
That was your biggest mistake.
I hope they don't come home now.
"Don't ever say sorry to anyone.
Don't bow your head unless they force you to.
And even then, even then think positive."

"I'm sorry alright?
What else can I say?
What more do you want?
You give birth to me then you want to bury me as soon as you can!"

"It's not my fault your friends slapped you!"

"They're not my friends! They're just people…just some people I know…"

She stares at me.

"Why don't you try and find better friends?"

"How? Where? Better friends don't exist."

"What about Russians? You said there is a Russian boy in your class."

"There is but he's an idiot."

"Why?"

"I don't know. I can't explain it."

"You need to give people a chance. Everyone's more or less an idiot."
I nearly had my eyes taken out.
I've been slapped and kicked and she says I need to give people a chance.

Bogdan Tiganov

"Come on…eat something at least."
I want to eat my heart.
I want to put it on a plate and stick my knife and fork into it.

★

"I'm going to kick their heads in. Who was it?"

She tells me.
I don't know them.

"I'm going to castrate them."

"You're going to do nothing!
Talk! Talk! You're all just mouth!
Useless words!
That's what we're satisfied with!
Empty, useless, pointless, stupid words!"

She just runs out like I knew she would.

This green bedroom is small.
I've seen much bigger.
I need bigger.
It becomes a jungle at night when the spiders run up and down the walls.
It's soothing, though, watching them travel endlessly across space, drifting from walls to floor and from floor to bed and then onto my arms.
They're my best friends.
Black and white and fluorescent yellow, small and growing and lifting tiny hairs.
Why did they paint it green?
I don't mind it, but why?
Lights off and papa's footsteps.
(I refuse to call him tata like the rest of them.)
His voice is like a smack in the gut.

The Wooden Tongue Speaks

He's still alive.
Fucker just won't die even with all the cars and buses and trams that could run him over, or holes in the ground that he could snap his neck in.
And when he gets home he does this, that's the way he is with the bones sticking out of his face.
He has to slam the door.
He had to break the chain off last month when mama locked him out.
He's exploding and it's been happening for years.
He's been terrorizing us.
That's what it is, with all the love in the world.
Oh yeah, that's what it is.
Love.
Undoubtedly.
It's difficult for him as it is for us.
More difficult.
What would we know?
Nobody can know anything about anybody else.
We just sit here guessing.
Angry.
Very much so.
A passion for learning and a good job.
If you can't get what you want get prepared to buy it.
And you can only afford it if you've spent the time learning what you need to.
Not art.
Not writing.
Not music.
Not football as football is for illiterate idiots.
Not tennis.
That's what he tells me.
Mathematics.
Science.
Get it stuck in your head and don't ever let it leave.
The tone of voice.
Repetition.

Bogdan Tiganov

And angry.
And his tone goes up so we hear it.
They don't care about that.
One day, one day I'll get my own back.
The swearwords and insults, this marriage.
But what about my marriage?
What will mine be like?
How will I treat my family?
Can a man understand everything he needs to before it's too late?
She's right.
I mean it is just talk isn't it?
Like scratching ourselves to death, endlessly repeating the same dreams
and we can't escape the cycle no matter what we do.
Let's run.
Let's go somewhere else.
Suicide.
Not the answer.
Give me an answer.
God.
That's why I pray to you.
For an answer.
An answer to everything.
God.

★

"Vali?"

"Present."

"Vali?"

"Yes sir?"

"At your age it's unwise to be so serious.
You'll get frowning lines on your face."

The Wooden Tongue Speaks

They laugh at me.
Can't imagine anything crueler.
His stupid face like a punch bag there to be pummeled.
And what's happening to my heart and why am I going red in the face again?
Just sit and swallow.
Everybody does it.
He says you've got to take it.
But he also says hit back, hit back as hard as you can.
Anytime.
When they're waiting for it or when they're not expecting it.

"Yes."
No!

★

"Look at her face. Do you think this is acceptable?"

"Of course not. But what can I do?"

"What can you do?
Do your job…phone their parents, get them down here and I'll talk to them if you can't.
Don't put your job on the line. I'll do it."

"I can't do that."

"What did you say?"

"I said I can't do that. Now go. Luiza will be alright."

"Listen, dickhead, pick up the phone and do your fucking job.
Pick it up now or I'll pick it up for you!"

His voice is so high it's embarrassing.
He's fuming and his hands are clenching the table like a vice.

Bogdan Tiganov

What will he do?

"You want me to call the police?"

"And what the hell will you do then?
Pay them off to shut their dirty mouths?"

"Don't be rude."

Quiet.
He leans back in his chair.
The headmaster's relaxed.
Papa looks at me, red in the face.
Angry as hell.
We'll get it later, his frustration.

"Let's go."

I am half my size.
I am disappearing.

"One day I'll come back and burn this fucking school down."

★

My reputation is on the line so no wrong moves from now on.
No mistakes allowed today.
Sometimes, you can smell the sweat, seeping through from the pores.
You can smell the problems, the tension created by time, the cannibals.
Yes.
The sweat, the shit.
Don't be scared.
Don't shake.
Look straight ahead and aim.

"Hey! What the fuck!"

The Wooden Tongue Speaks

Just hit.
He's moving.
Get closer.
He's fat.
Tall.
He's not going down.
Aim and hit.
The mouth, teeth.
Make him bleed.
Make him pay.

"Get him!"

"Russian idiot!"
"Ruskie prick!"

"Look, Adi! That's the way they fight in Russia!"

Can't hear.
Let's finish this.
Forget the left, lean on the right.
Move your legs.
Take his legs out.
What?
Cowards.
Bastards.
Don't stab people in the back.
Go straight for the face.
Breathe.
Concentrate.
You can't lose.
It's impossible.
If they do that you must respond.

"I'll get my knife."

"No."

Bogdan Tiganov

"Knife the Ruskie!"

"Shut up."

They've got me.
Control.
It's what they like, what they're used to, nothing new for them.
The group.
Struggle.
Fight.
Don't let them win.
Don't cry or look down.
With their knees, their fists, elbows, they can't bring me to where they want me.

"He's crazy!"

"Look at his eyes!"

The Poet of a Thousand Love Poems

When they got in the car it was something.
The old women with scarves wrapped round their heads, bent backs,
they're exquisite but they're not here now.
The old men throwing their dice in the park, it's the morning routine to
figure out who's king of the numbers.
Keep the young ones off the streets.
Their blonde heads, their brunette heads love to dance and skip.
Bring them inside.
Let them tease the animals, climb trees, let them dig for life.
Zaharia didn't drive.
He didn't have the money to learn and didn't really want to risk it.
He would have to, sometimes, to prove his bottle.
Then his left knee shook slightly but he did it with a brave face.
He was good looking, but nothing special.
And he was surprised that Angela liked him.
Angela was one of the most beautiful girls in school.
Boys fought for her.
Boys got on their knees for her.
They prayed to God so she would touch them.
When you saw her, first, there wasn't anything stunning.
Then she would, then she would move.
Her slightly reddish curls would move.
It was like silk.
It was like the rain, from behind to front, more here, less there.
And her tiny face would eventually look at you, and her eyes would grow
before yours, her face shaped in front of you, as if God was showing
exactly what he could do.

Bogdan Tiganov

That mouth, pink and red and shaped like a slice of an autumn apple.
She became and she took you over.
She surrounded you and you no longer existed.
This happened to Zaharia and he would look for and at her whenever he could, in class, during lunch, after class he would watch her legs support and grace that svelte body away.
When he prayed at night he couldn't quite get her out of his mind.
He kept trying to think about God, about Jesus, and the good things that everyone deserved, health and prosperity.
These thoughts disappeared fast and instead he would rotate Angela in his mind.
In his mind she was his doll.
He could flip her, he could undress her.
And what he couldn't understand was why she wasn't going out with anybody.
Maybe she was.
Maybe it was a rich old guy.
A film star.
One of the smooth-talking gangsters on TV.
So what?
Did she think she was too good for them?
How can anyone be so arrogant?
How can anyone be so beautiful?
Then they started going out.
It happened like this: she came to him at lunch and said
"I like that poem you wrote."
The poem she referred to was so bad he couldn't believe he'd written it.
It was about God and the country but it had secret bits in it.
Bits about her.
She said "I like that poem you wrote" and then it was easy because she became human.
Two nights later they kissed by the old clock and he felt her hair and he felt her back and he felt like he would die right there by the old clock, that blue clock.

When they got in the car it was something.
Radu was the funniest guy you're likely to meet.

The Wooden Tongue Speaks

He was a caricature, with his elastic face that he could twist like a clown.
He played them the latest tunes from Greece and Italy while they kissed in the back seats.
Radu was also the best driver.
He was better than their fathers.
Their fathers could never pull off those moves, swinging the car from side to side, just missing incoming lorries, at incredible speed, always at incredible speed.
You couldn't believe that car was capable of such speed.
It was blue.
It had been blue.
But the rust was burning it.
It looked like a sad cardboard box but when Radu moved it, well, he moved it, from side to side, overtaking everything, carts and sports cars and everything.
Move.
When there was a straight road with nothing on it the car felt like it would explode.
Take off.
Boom.
Further and faster.
Radu was a good friend.
You should've seen the smile on his face when fat middle-aged businessmen swore at him.
You should've heard him laugh when mothers, holding on to their children with overprotection, struck him horrified looks.
All this while the couple kissed in the back seats, whispering to each other, promising each other miracles, they would move, they would travel, they would see and experience, they would learn and work, they would get ok jobs just to get by and they would live somewhere scenic and there raise their family, one boy and one girl.
Their children would play, free, and wouldn't have to work.
It was late and Radu was driving them home.
He wasn't going fast.
It was steady pace.
His lights were too dim so he didn't see the bike.
He did see the bike and when he saw it it was too close he swerved and

Bogdan Tiganov

the brakes couldn't hold.
The brakes could hold but he still had his other foot on the accelerator.
Move.
The car crashed into a tree, its back lifted off the ground.
When the impact happened Radu no longer smiled and the couple were no longer kissing in the back seats or promising each other miracles.
Radu smashed through the window, his body flipped several times and fell with a thump.
Nobody was wearing seatbelts.
Radu was too good a driver for that.
They had complete faith in him.
Zaharia got bashed into the seat in front and his face crushed into the wheel and his legs snapped.
He saw her as her head got hammered by whiplash
and bone met hard plastic.
There was no wheel there where she was.
And her position was unnatural.
Her arms and legs were curved into the seat and her sublime hair covered her face.
That's what he remembered.
That's when she died.

*

Radu was fine.
In fact, he had no injuries to speak of.
Just a few scratches.
Zaharia wasn't.
He couldn't walk for half a year and he was on morphine.
When he was conscious he wasn't conscious for long because he had terrible attacks of madness and violence.
He would scream.
He wanted to kill Radu, he would never forgive him, he couldn't forgive them, he couldn't do that, it was too late now, he wanted to kill him, he wanted to kill himself.
He would go red and blue and violet in the face and his family were really sad for him.

The Wooden Tongue Speaks

They were glad he was alive.
But he wasn't glad.
He realized that he couldn't live without her so he raged and raged and raged until he passed out.

It was a year later that he went back to school.
He was seventeen.
He came in and sat down.
He didn't see anybody.
He didn't see Radu.
He didn't see the teacher's look of pity.
He'd let his hair grow.
He hadn't cut it at all.
It was curly and brown and it covered his whole face.
Nobody had hair like that in school.
They were told to get it cut after a couple of weeks.
He walked with a slight limp.
He walked nice and straight.
But he never looked at you in the eyes.
Zaharia was having morphine withdrawal and he felt he couldn't survive without it.
He felt he needed it to dull his pain.
He didn't care about his appearance or his family or school.
But he did the work and the school year went well.
And he had no friends until he met Bogdan.
Bogdan got on well with everybody.
He had a likeable face and he was easy going.
He was not particularly good at anything but nobody messed with him because he had friends in high places, and that means you mess with me you get your windows broken and you get your car busted and you may even get yourself done in one night when you're feeling relaxed coming home late.
Not even the gangs messed with Bogdan.
He could go wherever he wanted untouched.
He had a nice friendly face and he wore glasses and he was modest.
And what nobody knew was that Bogdan could appreciate and understand suffering.

Bogdan Tiganov

His parents were poor.
His girlfriend had breast cancer.

"So what do you like?"

"I don't know."

"Come on, you must like something."
"I don't."

Bogdan handed him another cigarette.
He thought that Zaharia was the best looking guy in school.
He looked incredible, with his hair and his tight bone structure and his red stubble.

"I like to write."

"Oh yeah?"

But Zaharia stopped talking and Bogdan decided not to ask anything else in case Zaharia got fed up with it.
This friendship was worth the struggle.
A couple of weeks passed.
After school, walking home, Zaharia palmed Bogdan what looked like fifty sheets of paper.

"Is this your writing?"

Zaharia didn't look at him and didn't answer.
They went home.
Bogdan went straight to his room.
He threw himself on his bed and he looked at the papers, handwritten in blue ink.
He read twenty pages.
Poems.
He had dinner.
Then he read the other thirty pages.

The Wooden Tongue Speaks

Zaharia kept handing him poems every week.
Bogdan read them, every line, every word.
He'd never read so much in his life.
He'd read Eminescu and he'd quite enjoyed it.
Zaharia was better.
These poems changed the way you felt.
They brought tears to your eyes or a smile to your face and you could understand them.
He was quick to spread the word.

"You're a genius."

"No. I just write love poems."

"You should let other people see them."

"No."

So Bogdan showed them.

Girls used to dream about him, this mysterious handsome poet who was always thinking about his dead girlfriend, how romantic and heart breaking.
He wasn't interested in any of them.
They were false.
They were boring.
They had no life.
He was interested in writing.
He spent his time indoors.
He did his homework and projects and he would write from eight to twelve when he would try again and again to sleep.
He wrote thousands of poems.
He knew the words.
They just came out right.
He could feel them in the right place, rhyme or no rhyme, the words felt correct.
He could associate them with imagery and, with practice, the imagery

Bogdan Tiganov

and words began to flow out together.

His hair came to halfway down his back.
His beard was quite advanced too.
He had smoky green eyes but you hardly got to see them.
He spent his time with his only friend, Bogdan.
They would sit by the fountain and talk and smoke.
At university he studied economics.
He was totally uninterested in it and the girls and the attempts from others at friendship.
He had three or four books written.
Three or four books of the best writing Bogdan had read or will read.
Bogdan's girlfriend lived through cancer.
Then they broke up and he started going out with a
damn good peasant girl.

Goodnight Work

A man got in and said he wanted to go to the old town.
He gave strange directions the driver didn't know.
It happened sometimes.
He was a taxi driver who waited daily by the hospital.
It was a good place to wait.
Sick people needed him.
But they didn't like paying.
A dying man preferred to walk home.
He worked seven days and five nights a week.
Cristi drove the man down dying streets.
The passenger wasn't drunk but he didn't speak.
It might have been an illusion but he was red in the face.
Cristi put the radio on to combat the silence.
On the radio there were manele[21] and people with excited voices.
It was one twenty-three in the morning.
People with excited voices and silence in the car.
It's an incredible feeling when you know that people are sleeping.
Drive through and they're in bed,
dreaming,
hugging,
kissing,
touching,
sleeping,
house after house,
one small and disfigured,
one newly built, plastic-like.

---

21 *Manele are musical amalgamations of Romanian and Eastern sounds, usually in bad taste.*

Bogdan Tiganov

The idea was to work long hours, make money and send it to his daughter. She needed it for university and he'd already sold most of his valuables, like the gold ring he'd received from his own father.
He didn't particularly like driving.
He'd been an engineer but the plant got closed down.
Many of his engineer friends were taxi driving.
He didn't smoke.
He'd quit.
He liked a drink with his meal, but only one drink.
This man wasn't well dressed.
In fact he was wearing a vest and old trousers with paint on them.
And he had body odor.
Cristi had a pleasant face, thin but easy to look at.
He had a handsome gray moustache that went well with the rest of his face.
He was too thin and he knew it.
He loved his food but he couldn't gain in weight.
It was the metabolism.
His thoughts were something like
'Why is he wearing a vest in this weather?'
and 'This town breeds crazy people.'

"Have you ever been to Belgium?"
It was a shocking question to be asking a taxi driver after a difficult period of silence.

"No."

"Have you been anywhere in Europe?
I mean have you seen anything else apart from this town?
Like Belgium?"
This man was crazy.
His haircut was bad, crazy.

"No. I've never been to Belgium. I've never been to Europe."

"Oh," and he continued to look out the window.

The Wooden Tongue Speaks

"Oh," he said again.

Cristi wanted to get rid of the crazy man so he put his foot down.
It was an old house.
They didn't build them like that anymore.
But it hadn't been taken care of.
It was lived in to extremes.

"Wait. I'll be right back,"
and he gave Cristi some money.

Now Cristi would normally say "Don't worry you can pay me at the end"
but he didn't.
And he wanted so much to say he couldn't wait, that he had to go somewhere, but he couldn't lie.
He needed the money.
Before, as a younger man, he couldn't get up as easily.
There were more friends.
There was more talking.
It was hard work, much harder than driving a taxi.
And there were bosses.
Various bastards.
One was his friend.
One boss.
Doru.
He had great spirit.
Typically Moldovan[22].
And they liked a drink.
They liked to laugh.
Doru was tough when he had to be but he would bring a bottle of wine and they would have a couple of glasses when no one was looking.
There were some good times.
Yes, he remembered their conversations.

"My wife's useless. She can't do anything," one would say and the

---

22 *Moldova is a country bordering Romania. Its population speak Romanian as well as Russian and many Moldovans relocated to Romania to earn more money.*

Bogdan Tiganov

other would agree and it went on like "Guess what my boy's doing? Art!
The idiot will get nowhere with art!"

Cristi saw the man leaving the house, or trying to.
It looked like he was attempting to brush off his wife who was hanging on
to him and there was shouting.
Family problems.
The man slapped the woman off and swore at her and she swore back and
slammed the door.
He walked, determined, and got in.
Cristi turned to look at him.
He had horror on his face, sinews and sweat.
No man should ever have to look like that.

"Right. Let's go," said the man.

"Where?"

He told Cristi.
And he told him to keep calm.
He liked him the way he was.
Calm.
He didn't like him any other way.
He didn't like him asking questions.
He didn't like him thinking stupid things.
It wasn't far.
The house was up to date.
Large.
The color was peach.
He couldn't wait to get out.
He pushed the gate and bashed the doorbell.
Cristi saw his gun.
It wasn't much of a gun but it was a gun.
Any thoughts he had were gone.
Anything he might have said or done was over.
This man was going to shoot.
That's where the whole night was leading to.

The Wooden Tongue Speaks

And another man appeared from the background while Cristi was looking and looking.
The new man was fat.
He was tall.
The crazy man turned to look at the tall, fat man and then turned back.
The door opened.
A man with ruffled hair opened it.
He also was wearing a vest.

"You idiot!"

"I can't take this, I just can't, not one more second…"

"Give me that gun," and the tall man walked up to the crazy man who wasn't aiming his gun.

The man who'd opened the door looked like he didn't know what to do.

"Give me that gun!"

Cristi kept looking.
He'd been an honest man.
He'd never cheated anybody.
He even insisted the police pay their fare.
Yes he'd seen guns before.
He saw them in the so-called Revolution.
He saw somebody's father get shot.

"I'm sorry, Remus. I'm sorry. Let's talk."

"I can't talk. You don't deserve it," and his gun arm rose slightly.

"You idiot! You don't know anything!"
and the tall fat man got closer.

To Cristi it seemed a very long time.
There was no wind, no creatures, nobody else.

Bogdan Tiganov

He gripped his wheel.
Then he couldn't see properly because they had their back to him.
The three men were together and something was going on.
They went inside.
They closed the door.
He wondered what to do, whether a gunshot would come.
It would.
It had to turn this night into murder.
So he waited.
The lights in the windows never changed.
Shadows flicked across once in a while.
It was a nice house.
He liked the peach.
He wanted a house like that, only with a great gate to keep out the world
and a lovely serious German shepherd dog.
The lights went out and he gripped the wheel even tighter.
The tall fat man opened the door, stepped out then shut it.
He came alone to the taxi.
Cristi opened the door.

"Don't worry about this.
It's best if you just forget it.
You must've been worried there, right?"
He had many wrinkles on his face.

"Yes, I'm not used to it."
Many lines.

"You did well. You did a good job."

He searched his pockets and finally came upon his wallet, which was small enough and black, pulled out a few notes, then a few more notes.

"Here. What's your name?"

"Cristi."

The Wooden Tongue Speaks

"Cristi, if I need a driver I'll know who to look for."

Like that he turned and left.
Cristi shut his door, counted his money and drove off.

There was snoring.
She was snoring, pleasant and deep.
She had her back turned and he could see her right shoulder, her right arm over the blanket.
She was his woman and she'd been through enough.
It was very late, so late he wondered whether it was worth it.
But he took off his jumper, then his shirt, then his vest.
Then he undid his belt.
The trousers fell easily.
He tried not to make a sound but she was tired so she didn't hear it.
He raised the blanket and pushed her a little so he could fit.
He turned on his side.
His heart was beating too much.
Cristi moved closer to his wife, to feel her flesh, a bit closer.

He'd driven a few from the hospital to their homes, and a couple of old ladies to the cemetery.
A car pulled alongside his.
The window rolled down.

"Remember me?"
It was the man with the gun.

"How's business today?"

The man with the gun was driving a brand new Daewoo.
He was smiling a tremendous smile.
His black hair was slicked back and Cristi smiled at him.

⭐
Cold

I got in shivering from nerves and shivering from cold.
It was minus fifteen.
I turned the key.
Nothing.
I cursed my luck and my life.
My wife came out.
I told her to get behind the wheel and to work it while I pushed.
She was still crying from the previous night.
She looked old and lonely.
I had no strength left but I was determined enough and the adrenalin kicked in.
What if the car died for good?
I couldn't even think about that.
If the car doesn't work I die.
Right here.
Dead.
I heard the engine.
It started creeping.
She got out, no words, and went back in, the wounded wolf, one more indignity.
Forget about the house.
I wished I was never coming back.
I thought I could die from the cold.
I would have to beg for more clothes.
I looked around like a madman.
Nobody. They're hiding behind trees, maybe behind derelict buildings.
Knock it down for God's sake and build something new, something that

The Wooden Tongue Speaks

we could use, cheap or, better still, free.
Where were they?
I had that feeling of inevitability.
I was at peace.
I felt calm, a frightening feeling, surely the wrong feeling while the car
fought with the ice trapped underneath.
I had no time to clear it.
There was snow all over the windshield.
I had cleared a big enough hole so I could see.
It was a hard job, hard enough to make my nails bleed.
I sucked on the blood.
It dried up.
I reached up for the pack of Marlboros.
I pulled on the wrapper with my teeth.
My teeth felt cold.
I pulled out a cigarette and lit it first time.
I usually flick the ash out the window but I couldn't afford to open the
window so the ash went everywhere.
No matter.
Don't delude yourself with cleanliness.
It's so peaceful driving when there's nobody else on the road.
No life.
I made a cocktail of solitude and tension.
I stared at Christ trapped inside plastic dangling in front.
I thought it's times like these when we really need you, when we look up to
the heavens and scream CHRIST HELP US NOW!
But you're perfectly still stuck in the icon.
Time had no meaning.
I heard the sirens.
I lit another cigarette.
I watched the bastard crunching through snow and hoped the snow would
suck him in to hell.
I pulled on my beard, analyzed myself.
My eyes were red with lack of sleep.

"Name?"

Bogdan Tiganov

"Mihai Enescu."

"Identity?"

I handed the murderer my life printed on a few flimsy pages, brown covers.
He stared at it as if staring at nothing.

"What are you doing out?
Where do you think you're going?
What about your fucking boundaries?"

"I need to get to Piatra Neamţ, my mother's very ill and she's got nobody."
He stared at me, nothing, and stared all around me.

"Ah…Marlboros…great American brand no?"

"That's right."
I handed him my pack.
He put it in his shirt pocket as if it were his.

"So…your mama…she's very ill…"

"That's right. I have to go. It's an emergency."

"An emergency eh? What's wrong with her?"
He didn't think it was an emergency.
He was ready to pull the gun on me.

"She's got a brain tumor."
He was ready to burst out laughing.

"Ok go, but Mihai, you fucking cockroach, you'd better learn from your mistakes."

He stared at me like he was my mother, father, teacher and God rolled

The Wooden Tongue Speaks

into one.
I nodded but I wanted to grab the bastard and strangle him, slice him up, feed him to the dogs.
He'd just come out of the army, no idea about life, having a bit of fun playing the power game.
I watched him march back to his car, a young Godless piece of shit.
Then I reached up for my second pack of Marlboros.
I tried not to think because thinking was dangerous.
They don't want you to think.
They want you to work.
They want bodies.
I saw no animals.
They were hiding.
Even the bears.
When I saw another car, a battered old gray Dacia with a battered old alcoholic inside, I looked away, couldn't face another person eye to eye.
What was he doing out?
Maybe he lived there.
I stopped soon after.
I felt like I was going to breakdown.
I started weeping.
Howling.
I was flattened by a moment of despair.
I found some coffee in the boot.
It was cold but I could still drink it.
I felt it going down through my system.
I smoked awhile, shivering, no more tears, there was nothing left, when you crash through insanity everything feels neutral.
I put on the radio.
I gave it a smack for effect.
Folk music, sad voices exclaiming happiness, everything's perfect, everything works, that's the message, don't let sadness get in the way.
I should've stayed abroad.
In Portugal where it's warm and civilized.
On the beaches where they drink wine and smoke freely.
On the beaches where it's free.
In the warm sunshine where the fish are easy and the women are pretty

and kind, where the people have the spark of life in their eyes.
I hit the radio again to shut its droning.
I saved some coffee for later.
I finished the cigarettes.
I drove until I saw the roadblock.
It was the alcoholic idiot who'd crashed into a tree.
His brains were on the windscreen.
They wiped him off into the woods and left him there and no one would miss him.
They probably shot him.
It didn't matter.
One of the official criminals ran up to me.

"What are you doing here? Get out!"

I got out, calm, fully in control of myself and of my frozen mind.
He searched me.
His face was like that of a wild boar.
His uniform stank of booze.
He insulted Brăila under his breath.
He led me to his car and barked at me.
I got in.
I watched them, four brutes, chatting, profiteering.
Two of them got in.
One of them went to my car and the other one I don't know.
I spoke a few words on the way but not too many words.
They led me to a room where they just left me to rot.
I said nothing to defend myself.
Shit and piss in the corner, rats waiting there, a dark room with no window and no toilet and no bed just the impression of light through the cracks, the dirt and dust between the cracks, tarnished iron and tarnished copper, no heating, food, drink or smokes.
I thought of my wife cursing me and cursing my parents, the little whore couldn't wait to get rid of me but I brought in good money, and my daughter trying to study through the tears.
I saw my house and all the work, the lifting, the plans, how good we felt when it was finished and tata celebrated in his usual style, by getting

The Wooden Tongue Speaks

paralytically drunk.
Tata, how much anguish he'd brought me.
He made good money but he blew it all on drink.
I looked through the cracks in the door.
Nobody.
I would have to wait.
Mama would have to wait.
I couldn't feel anything.
They came when I was feeling like a bird that doesn't realize
there's glass there.
My head against walls.
Door.
My hands were stuck inside my jacket as they dragged me to another room
with stronger lights and a five foot six weasel waited for me there.
I should've stayed in Portugal.

"Mihai...what did you see?"
I couldn't really focus my eyes and I had to stop myself from spitting
down his throat.

"See?"

"What did you see?"

"I saw nothing, I don't care, I need to see my mother and that's all I care
about. I need to see my mother."

"What did you see, Mihai?"

"I saw your mama, cocksucker!"

I felt the electricity shoot through me and then I saw the floor and spat
some blood on it.
They zapped me some more and then the weasel pissed on me.

"What did you see, Mihai?"

Bogdan Tiganov

"I saw…two cars…one had crashed…and that's it…"

He zipped up.
It wasn't too smart walking around with his dick out.
He offered me a cigarette.
I took it and smoked it.

"We'll drive you to your mother's and you'll do what you have to do and then we'll work it out."

I didn't understand.
I couldn't understand anything at the time.
I spat some more blood on the floor.
I threw the cigarette butt on the floor.
I followed two boars outside where it felt colder than before.
Once I got to the car, which happened to be my car, I passed out.

Mama was in a terrible state.
I gave her some money and told her she's coming home with me once the winter's over.
It was unlikely that she would make it through winter.
I also told her not to worry about me as I'm doing fine, the job's great, the wife's on the right track, the law loves me…
The boars took me to one side and told me I was a good man and they'd let me go.
They were impressed by the sight of my mother and they'd decided that I was reasonably innocent.
They left and smiled to mama with their gold teeth and wooden hearts.
I'll never forget the look of natural superiority they gave us.
I made some coffee and went to have a warm bath but left some blood on the coffee cup.

Green

If you want to talk politics, I'll talk politics.
If you want to make change happen you've got make slight sacrifices.
It's a trick, a pleasant illusion that works well if you've got the right timing and reasonably hard-working people involved.
People are constantly depressed.
They're feeling low because there's no work for them, because they can't pay the rent.
The prices go up but the salaries stay the same.
That's their problem.

"Do you ever notice anything when you're driving through town?"

"What do you mean?"

"Keep your eyes open.
They're not open.
They're stuck together with glue."

"Don't talk to me like that.
Just tell me what ideas you have."

"I'm sorry."
The clocks are ticking.
Mind metronomes.

"This town needs green."

Bogdan Tiganov

"Green."

"Grass. Flowers. Plants. Trees. Green."

"What for?"

"Happiness."
Another cigarette.
The coffee's finished.

"Then happiness is too expensive."

"It is the most expensive commodity in the world."

"Right."

"I'm glad you understand."

"I love your ideas.
You're a genius.
You've saved me again.
You're more than a friend to me you know that?
You're my most valuable employee."

They certainly brought in the manpower saying they're great horticultural experts from France when really they were second-rate actors with school-level French.
But they looked good in their second-hand suits.
And they certainly made an impression prancing around and sounding important.
Stupid as they were, though, they didn't care that at lunch they kept taking out bottles of beer and drinking.
People didn't question it.
Everybody needs a drink, especially important folk.

"What's with the French idiots?"

The Wooden Tongue Speaks

"They're working on changing the landscape."

"Unbelievable."

"The noise they make…"
"How can they possibly think we'll take it?
How can they do this to us?
How do we take it?"

"We just take it. I don't know how we do it."

"An idiotic nation. We're an idiotic nation with no character."

"What's wrong with you?
Why are you so upset?"

"They think they can trick us.
They think they can keep repeating the same illusion only grander.
I tell you I'm not voting.
I don't care if I end up in prison or deported or shot but I'm not voting."

"What are you talking about? Have a drink."

"I know what I'm on about. I don't need a drink to relax. I'm fine."

"You don't sound fine."

"I'm sick to death of my job. That's probably what it is."

"Yeah? Well I'm sick to death of mine but you don't hear me complaining."

"That's because you're perfect."

What they found was that you couldn't grow anything.
The ground was hard as nails and radioactive.
Amazingly, the worms were still struggling.

Bogdan Tiganov

Madness.
Only they didn't report the truth.
They said there might be a problem with the projected growth but they didn't say it was impossible because they figured they would get paid for something.
They continued planting seeds in dead ground.
And they overdid it.
They put so many seeds that if by some miracle the seeds would grow there would be no space for the plants to grow.
A great amount of beer was also consumed in order to make the whole situation feel less farcical.

"Mama?"

"Yes?"

"Why is the moon following me?"

"The moon is your friend."

"Oh."

"The moon will protect you wherever you are and the bigger it is the more protection it will give you."

"How far away is it?"

"Not that far."

"Mama?"

"Yes?"

"I don't understand. Why is the moon my friend?"

"Mama? What's that?"

The Wooden Tongue Speaks

"Yes?"

"What's that?"

It was something which made that mother and all the mothers and grandmothers and young thugs stop what they were doing.
Shopping bags and umbrellas and beer bottles hit the floor.
All around near the tram they saw what looked like shoots of bamboo and palm leaves and weeping willows growing at a speed they knew impossible, a speed so ridiculous their eyes had trouble keeping up.
The earth was producing.
The earth was making the impossible happen and nobody said anything.
It was growing without direction over and under the tram and growing so much they couldn't quite see beyond, whether the cars and blocks of flats were still there was left to their imagination.
The green had decided to take action.
There was so much of it that it egged itself on.
It decided to show what can be done.
Against all odds.
Against the impossible.

When he's asleep he has intricately detailed dreams that distort reality into a Cubist painting.
People get ill and their limbs fall off.
He feels great emotion and horror.
There is no rest…and if he'd known…what else could he have done?

"Yes?"

"Doctor, we have…something…here…"

"I was sleeping. Why the hell did you wake me up?"

"It's an emergency that's why!"

He is in a rush but his wife wouldn't care if he fell in a well and snapped his spine in two.

Bogdan Tiganov

And he is driving but he forgot his watch and mobile.
This is part of the job.
He is at their mercy.
He tightens his belt and swears.
Swearwords never lose their ability to motivate.

But now he is speechless.
He hadn't expected to feel so present as if a million arrows struck him into the spotlight.

"I think…it's vital we contain this story."

"We can't do that. The scavengers are getting ready to attack."

"Then we block off the roads and we block off the skies.
We tell them this is top secret.
We write out an urgent request and get it signed by the government.
We make out this is ours.
This is our atom bomb."

The streets overflowing with campanula romanica[23] were like one bed of freedom from dream world or heaven.
Through campanula romanica grew delphinium simonkaianum[24] and unbelievable purple graced through yellow and green.
And green my God green untouched by anything so majestic that people were afraid to reach out with their hands and touch it.
Nature was no longer something you bashed under your feet.
And somehow the drunk woke up where he was on the park bench and looked around him and vomited on himself for a great leaf had burst off through the cracks and was holding him right there in mid-air.

"Ion?"

"You know it's me. I don't have money to lend."

---

23 *Rare plant species.*
24 *Rare plant species.*

The Wooden Tongue Speaks

"Ion? I don't need it. I'm rich. I've got…everything…"

"I told you to stop drinking and stop calling me!"

"Come and have a look, come and have a look, come and have a look at my garden!" and she left the phone where it was, leaving Ion to scream into it on the other end, and she left it and went outside and her smile was astonishing for anyone who saw it, only nobody saw it and that's fine too. Then she opened her arms as if she were hugging her mama and jumped in. And now the mayor wasn't laughing. A spruce tree had grown across his windows, blocking his view of the Danube.
He couldn't see anything.
He noticed the doorbell ring.
His ashtray was full.
He noticed the ring and he thought for a moment he wouldn't move off his chair except to maybe light up another cigarette but he knew he would have to because whoever was ringing was probably angry and important and threatening, and the president was probably on the phone asking his people what the fuck was going on.

"Tame it."

"How? We don't have big enough tools."

"Bring out the old farming equipment. Fix it, oil it, and use it. Bring the tanks out and blow holes through it!"

"We'll try the farming stuff."

"You try it. Try. And start trying with that bastard tree!"

He pointed to his window.

Nothing was strong enough or powerful enough to smack down the spruce trees, the beech trees and oak.
And it kept growing back.

Bogdan Tiganov

And people would swear at you even though you were only
doing your job.
You hated to ruin their happiness but you were living through orders and,
after all, one of these things had smashed through your windscreen.
All work was crazy but this was crazy work.
Indeed, let them out from the asylum and they could do it blindfolded.
It broke your heart.
You'd never seen them so deliriously happy.
Not even after the so-called Revolution.

I'll talk politics.
I'm not frightened of consequences.
What happens is that eventually things fade, people forget naturally.
It turns into a story.
And then gossip.
Belief and disbelief.
Words.
Memories.
You've got to understand simple psychology.
The mind works in mysterious yet savage ways.
In politics you've got to understand the basics.
We're not all Jesus Christ and we can't all save the world.
That's what happens.
Through hard work and illusions, through suffering and happiness, comes
re-election.
Order.

End (Justice)

When he was a baby he was in need of care because his parents were too busy working, socializing, and working some more.
The work was as soul-destroying as it was backbreaking.
And when they got home they simply wanted to stab each other, for strangers love each other in crazy ways.
At Christmas, though, there were fleeting moments of tenderness.
When he was a baby he was pampered like a prince by his grandparents.
He realizes he was a very lucky boy.
Tataia came and watched him and talked to him and told him about the world.
His baby blue eyes and the rest of him were calm, not like when hearing his parents screaming.
Mamaia came to cook for him and everyone else.
After retiring she would get up very early to cook for them.
She would get up extremely early to wait in line for milk and bread.
It was a very long line to wait in.
When he got a bit older he sometimes waited in or near the line with her.
Humans are not made for endurance.
Their systems are much too sensitive.
Mamaia also read to him and kissed him and talked to him sweetly.
He didn't understand everything but he understood her love. It was open, giving and forgiving.
So, while tataia taught him how to react mamaia taught him how to love.
In fact, as a teenager he would feel so much love for his parents and their struggles that he would try everything he could to please them, to see them smiling.
It was almost impossible.

Bogdan Tiganov

Her love was not something that changed.
Nothing in the world could change it.
A totalitarian system couldn't destroy it.
They tried everything they could to turn people into machines.
But they just couldn't turn true love into grease oil.
This fact is a problem for any dictator because without true love there is no growth and eventually everything rots.
Holes begin to appear and no amount of egotism will prevent the holes from taking over.
The show crumbles.
One moment you're in the grandest palace on Earth, bathing in gold, the next you're six feet under in the palace of dung.
Love is our gift as human beings.
When he started school he was ready to deal with kids.
They're like wild animals and you tame them by showing no fear and fighting back.
It's a game of territory.
There are a few nice kids.
They can be fun and lively and great companions.
Kids are great Romantics, great at melodrama.
One friend wanted them both to slice their hands and press their bloody gashes together.
Friends forever.
He did get in trouble a few times.
That's what happens when you fight back.
Justice turns its head and laughs at you.
Only mamaia came to school and told everyone that he was the most angelic most hard-working child.
Just take a look at his grades! Perfect! Just listen to him play piano!
They had to agree that he was indeed a special child who could do no wrong.
They would, instead, have to punish the others and justice smirked.
What she did, really, was to cover him in a cloak of love so he didn't feel the potentially head-busting problems.
She became his mama when his mama went to work abroad.
Tataia was a better father figure than his tata. He was honest, straightforward, inventive and intelligent.

The Wooden Tongue Speaks

He taught him that being a man means to offer your chin to the world and
not flinch when the strike comes.
Circumstances change though, things move on, things come, things go.
He no longer had his cloak of love.
It was a new world to bounce off.
New gray walls to make the heart surrender.
Without the cloak the fight gets tougher.
It gets unbearable.
He must face isolation.
He must face fear of failure.
Disease comes and no doctor can tell you why.
It rubs off sparks and consumes.
It multiplies and overwhelms.
There is no advance warning only an inevitable reminder of mortality.
In his branded isolation he loses his father figure who'd taught him to
read, who'd taught him the importance of courage and, most importantly,
to laugh even when problems are burying you because life's a whore.
He went to see tataia laid out in a coffin.
There were old women and relatives around tataia, crying and praying.
Now they loved him.
They hated him when he was alive because he told them how it was.
Justice pulls tight its impenetrable blindfold.
Years pass and tataia lives strong.
He strides through the mist.
The losses keep coming as justice pisses on the good.
Two great friends die, one taken by loneliness, alcohol,
the other by old age.
Disease comes and no doctor can tell you why because people shy away
from responsibility.
Child, the whys are many and brutal.
Because there was stress which made you cry and cry and cry, stress that
you couldn't share because others had their own stress pinning them
down.
Because you were eating food so old and green Western animals wouldn't
touch it.
Because there was no end to your work, inhaling chemicals and then

home where you cleaned everything by hand, on your knees you wiped the floors over and again.
Because there was not enough appreciation.
Everyone thought that's what women are supposed to do, a quick sleep and on your feet again for eighteen hours, endless and unfair.
Justice knows despite its continued cold gaze.
Because you missed your family and there was nothing you could do about their suffering and this inability to help got you down.
Because of the nuclear radiation and experiments.
Because your organism was simply too fragile to take on so much.
And so the good are beaten and their love flayed while the bad don't stand trial.
Justice is teaching us an ironic lesson.
The love of the few helps to flourish the hate of the many.
This is the way it ends.
Justice turns its ugly head and sighs.
But, we keep at it.
We get up, we dress, we walk, we do our business.
Some prefer to fit in snug with constancy.
They have their moments of doubt.
Some prefer to hit out.
Miniature rebels.
They also have their moments of doubt.
Punching a brick wall can hurt.
Some prefer to care deeply, living through the heart.
God bless them – love, the creator of evolution.

Poetry

HOME

Home's like, home's like this
Walking down streets gypsies on
Street corners chasing me
Wanting a lock of hair for good luck.

Home's like, home's like you see it,
Driven round in the pick of stolen cars
Hey there's my villa, fifteen levels,
Fifteen gold rings on one finger, gangsters?
All my relatives small-time hustlers.

Home's like, home's a dreamland
And I can't leave it
In the spring when the flowers are in bloom
I'm thinking the flowers just aren't mine
And when I'm home these flowers just don't
Want
Me.

Home's like, home's an empty restaurant
Where we eat the very best
And we drink only five star wine, flashing
Western cash, they're waiting for me outside
For an autograph – sign it in dollars.

Oh, it's beautiful, it is

Being here so carefree, beautiful to reminisce,

Make up fantasies which suit.

Home, after all, is a cement zone, a hit and run,

An escape pod, an alternative mindset and

A reason to feel better

Or worse.

⭐

PATRIOTISM

Like babies

We stare at the flags

And beat our hearts

With patriotism.

We pretend that

Nobody else exists,

That we can just

Leave it,

That money

Grows on God's beard.

And like babies

Our naive eyes

And our kitten mouths whisper

"Is that what we do?

Is that what we're supposed to do?"

I SEE THE LIONS

We went in
And it wasn't too frightening
Because we were all in it
So I didn't even notice
The lions.

We went in
Laughing,
Sometimes
Crying.

I thought this was paradise.

I took it for granted.

I thought I deserved
Some
Happiness.
I thought I had
It –
Others said I was naive
And inexperienced –
I laughed at what I thought
Petty.

And then they disappeared.

Everybody.

Gone.

For the first time
I saw the lions
I saw the lions I saw the lions for the first time
It hit me bludgeoned me hammered destroyed me.

I looked round me and asked "Doesn't anybody care?"
But there was no audience.
No judge.

There was me
And the lions devouring me.

★

THE HIDDEN DEPTHS

Where're you from?
London, Brăila,
UK, Romania,
No that would be simple
And unpoetic.

I am from a broken arm

Your father's in fact,
Stitched behind my back –
I'll keep it there
Alright?
You can do with me
As you the dog.
Let him drag himself
Chained-up to the water bowl,
His eyes
Are
Far kinder than mine,
Browner, sadder, more poetic
Yes,
That's where I'm from –
From a drunken soldier's
Open hand, earthen,
Dusty, crumbling,
A beggar's hand,
A lover's hand
Bruised and cut,
Dead yet not
Bleeding.

Now,
What're you hiding?

NICU

You were the best poet I heard.

It was an honor to be near you
And be taught by you. You need three things
To live well: a good heart, a trained mind, and
A gut paved with metal.

Nicu, today I sing about you again.

Nobody else could turn sixty years
Of suffering
Into humor.

YOUR WALK

A man must take
His last walk
But did you notice it?
Did you know?
Or
Did you step down
And your insides
Said

That's it?

Goodbye.

You called out for somebody!
Your family were far, too far
While I loved you like a father
And some kid talked to you
Thinking democracy is
Vandalism.

I
Should've
Driven you
To Europe,
Shown you
What you read of,
Dreamt of

But
No,
You took
Your
Walk
The
Walk
Took
You

THE HOUSE WE BUILT

We built the house
To what we need:
A room to sleep in,
A room to laugh in,
A room to eat in,
And the room to
Do what's necessary.
We wanted the garden
To be ours.
And we left our house
Where it was built
And we didn't come back.
We left it there strong
And beautiful, with the
Animals and trees.
But there's always a way back
If you find the path
Through my heart. Look
Carefully, we laughed
Like children and we
Laughed like angels and
We thought like
Intelligent bulls can.
In the house we built.

BEFORE WAKING

I tend to ignore breathing,
The dream's gone,
Fiction can hallucinate
Vancouver and Mexico City
At seven a.m. Twickenham,
And I don't know anything,
Not much, not worth repeating,
And nobody minds, it's normal.
Before lunch with
Always the wrong moment
And a big sandwich
That I can't ever swallow.
Before bed terrorized with sadness,
Of course.

SPIRITUALITY

You are this moment
A clear day
Your favorite
Spring
Summer
Burnt red
And a snowflake

On either cheek

This is spirituality

This moment
We've learnt out lessons

Every
Word

★ MEETING

At the bus stop
It never stops.
Only we stop.
Only he smiles at me
With a tearful sadness
And I don't smile back
With a friendship hatched
Of hatred.
He looks at me like a madman
On a cross. I stare back
Blank like the cross wearing
The madman.
He has his back bent
Fighting an invisible chair.
Mine is straight

In-between a vice coming
And staying.
There is no sound.
The sound of a pure ending.
He got on his bus.
He went on his way.
He didn't look back.
I stayed awhile longer.
I got on my bus.
I looked forward.

★

VISION

Don't struggle.
Hawks,
Their tender eyes
Like saints.

You can't go back
From the truth
Healthy and in
Working condition
Your pick-axe chipping away,
Slowly burning the line
That you can't change
And you can't see.

I thought it was a matter of

Waking up and turning up

But first you're mad

With the terrible eyes of vision.

THE KNOWLEDGE

I'll never know exactly the age that I've lived in

How right or wrong these years are

And who I am in a concrete garden

Is a mystery to me, and to you,

But maybe the gods know best

When man thinks he is his own devices.

I'll never know what you were like before we met

How innocent or valuable

And who was I before you?

A silent nod, we were gone,

But maybe the gods do know best

Or the greenery, or the insects…

WHEN I WAS A...

When I was a child
A long time ago,
When I was learning
To talk
I was thinking
Life is beautiful
And the world is endless
And there's never enough time…

When I was a child
I was so so
Happy
And
I was oh no
Sad
And I used to laugh forever
Till my ribs were in pain
When I was a child,
A long time ago…

When I was a child,
You know before all that
Bullshit,
When I had the time,
When tiredness was a concept,

Maybe I was wrong then –
And where's it all gone to now?
Maybe I can take it with me,
Maybe I can remember the truth
With this poem.

★

PRAYER

Help me, guide me,
A vision untoward
More glass than stained
More perfect than pained.
Teach me, show me,
An attitude correct,
Sever and dissect
Mold from bread,
Comfort purebred.
Create me on fire
Lighting alert
Revive my weary legs
Please
Stroke this heart of stone.
Forgive what is gone
Talent that burns
The altar of bone
Teach me, forgive me,
My childhood of home.

SPARROW

I held the sparrow in my little child's hand.
Fluttering.
Struggling.
Its eyes looked up asking
What are you doing here?

I don't know.

I felt its beating heart thumping against its layers
And mine.

Then I opened the door wanting
To keep the bird locked up with me forever.

CHILD

I am a child
And am ashamed of that and of the fear
I hold for mistakes, fear of failure and success,
Fear of lies and fear of truths,
Fear of everything and fear of you.

I get emotional when I visualize you
Because a poet does not write he breathes,

As I sit on my chair made for Emily Dickinson
And the blood of humanity pours from our ears
Only we can't feel that –
Too difficult to feel.

And as a child I see things differently
Through a mosaic, a Roman mosaic,
Crushed by my grandfather into
Lovely golden dust. A child is a child forever.

I don't know what to do. You tell me if it's clear
And thorough and paranoid I'll follow.
But I want to writhe round on the floor
Screaming and wring your neck,
Also.

⭐

CROW

Crow,

I will

Live

Longer than

You.

I will kill

Wheat.

I will snap

Sparrows.

I will sunrise.

I will sunset.

★

NEXT TIME

Guide me towards
Vethood – this time
I was wrong and lazy
And worked for nothing
But myself – next
Time I'd like to
Read the crooked
Leg of a barking
Bitch – guide me
Less stern, less well,
Tell me what I now know
Too late and too much.

★

NICHITA

You look overweight unprepared for a photograph.
You look disheveled
Posing for a magazine.
You look like a drunkard
Alive to sentimentality now

You look proud wearing
A cracked leather jacket
Your father forgot behind
For you to re-cry memories.
Your gray eyes now
They stare like ice blue
Vodka.
Staring away to a cement reminder of mortality…
And who bled you? Who
Reinvented mathematics?
Failing his Nobel,
Painting his underwear red,
Shot you in sepia
Looking like a man not a child,
Like a wolf like a lion,
Like you're unsure the
Dimension to carve up
And when but now
Your cheeks, wet, ballooned,
Wept demons and spread
Wings over black walls.

★

NATURAL CONCRETE

The goat disliked me
Pressing its hooves down behind
And bending its knees as if,

God I'm too young –
Now you take me for a city kid
With my middle-class accent,
LCD, navigator and gold chains,
But back then –
Back then rabbits hid red eyes
And chickens flocked aplenty
(Like yours, just like these)
Crested and dangerous –
Will your monster dog swallow me
Whole? I tried sleeping in a smelly room
With dark rugs on walls, dressed up
In their pajamas, "Where's
My nane[25]? My nane!" They didn't have it,
Sure, "There's this towel…"
I turned away, twisting
A mind weapon through
Hoarse a throat.
But, even then there wasn't enough,
You were talking, I, running,
Now I'm supposed to be –
Be in conversation,
Feeding the starving God of gossip
With poverty,
Lies –
The blind/deaf/quiet
Pants under the table in shade.
Waits.

---

[25] *Comfort blanket.*

UNHAPPINESS

Is as reasonable as
Happiness.

After all,
The sunset is just as
Beautiful
As the sunrise.

BEFORE I WAS BORN

I remember very clearly the day I was born,
Before no. It was an in-between moment
That day. In-between morning and lunch.
It was noisy and stressful only
We didn't think of it as stress.
Soon after it was finished at home
People flocked to me like they do
To a boss, any boss.
They talked to me and smiled at me
And imagined what would happen.
Every day.
A great family molding my blood
Through their fingers.

BUFFALO MILK

He said
"You can't stuff straw into
A machine and produce
Buffalo milk! That
You can't do!"

Your grandfather is ridiculously right.
We can, on the other hand,
Wipe out the universe.

DUST

The dust is ashamed
Bumped up driven –
What a time when Woody
Guthrie snuffed and spat
Back up protest –
Vengeance under layers
Of unspoilt ignorance,
Goneaways, profiteers, the
New Kings –
I distrust the free and
The carefree,
Nothing worse

Than being right,
The meek shall inherit the Earth
And the rest will own it –
The dust, the dust in the courtyard,
On the carpet, on our sandals,
Being swept away
To the same place it returns,
Tackling boxes
By covering thorns.

THE MOST BEAUTIFUL VERSE

The most beautiful verse is uncalled for,
Unnecessary, unexpected, as crazy
As blood from your nose.

It's cheating nature,
Stealing from the underside of a swan,
Whispering/screaming through
Jagged wooden cracks.

The most beautiful verse
Or
My wife, sleeping in the bed
Her grandfather built,
Looking as if
Cradled in her mother's womb.

I WISH

I wish

Life

Had a

Pounding

Drum beat

In the background.

I wish

Nights

In the country and

Jim Morrison's

Voice whispering

From branches.

I wish

Working

Days

Punctured

With a

Wailing

Hendrix solo,

The meaningless

We do

Combined

With

Valid

Death-defying

Naivety.

⭐

AN INSPIRATION TO MANY

Every time I unzipped a bag,
Searched through my pockets,
Pulled out a book or electric gadget,
Their eyes fixed from nowhere
To me.
How important and powerful was I!
A subject worthy of careful inspection
And consideration.
Why, indeed, bother writing?
I hope their grandchildren
Won't forget the novel I pulled out the bag.
I hope my mysterious gaze and scribbling
Will inspire the conversation of thousands.

⭐

THE ANGEL, THE EGG AND I

The angel sat in the kitchen smoking his cigarette
Seeing himself stood up earlier, sat down,

Walking off, wasting time, feeling sick,
Laughing with some devil.
He sits there, as I write this, sane but controlled,
Looking at the geometry of nothing,
Appreciating the genius of creation
Though there's a song he can't remember
With his mouth now full of drink.
Do angels need company? Or tragedy?
Who knows in a room as smoky as this.
I'm doing all the talking and the angel simply
Shuts the door. Same with the window.
He is not innocent.
He is not who he says he is.
He is a monster. A laughing lunatic.
I'll give him that room. He can have it.
I don't need anything anyway.
The angel sat there while the bombs went plop.
He laughed then, this so-called angel
As the brains went plop.
And as the bombs went plop and the brains followed suit
The angel sat in my kitchen chain-smoking through his pack
Collecting the ash in his left hand.
He smokes through a slit in his neck
As his mouth's stuffed full of lies.
I keep telling him, I kept telling him…
The buildings go phew
As the neighbors disappear to the sound of bop.
What are you laughing at you cancerous wreck?
You think I am joking? Fine, forget about me,

Concentrate on the egg. It's finally hatching.
The damn thing's been waiting for the bombs to go plop,
The brains to go top, the buildings to go phew,
And the neighbors, God forgive them, shop.
They're too busy for the hatching egg.
The angel gives it a kick, takes his halo
And smashes it to pieces against the egg
Then lights another cigarette.
Well, that didn't work, did it?
Here, give me one of those, I say,
But he opens the pack and there's none left.
There's no chair to sit on as the egg occupies one
And the angel the other. No cigarettes, no chair,
No alcohol and no air. That's the way it is.
The story of my life. A tragic comedy.
Show not tell. And this angel, you know,
Cares not for me, or you, or the egg.
If this is the afterlife…

★
NEEDS

She said you don't need friends, friends serve as backstabbing traitor
Bastards when you least expect them, always be aware awake
And don't let anybody know what you think what you want and
What you plan, keep it close to you and don't give it them –
Satisfaction, it's a game we're playing they're playing you play
Too you can't help that you'll see

And I saw, felt and we're taking the pills we find and we drink
The blood inside sucking up inside the heart, saving it for the needs
Of the poor and sitting in this boat watching the water come
And thinking about the sex in the book
And I felt, saw the banal bitch teacher wannabe penny-scraping
Architects of civilization collecting feathers to weigh down any lightweight
Brainwave, innocence and prevention of principle gathering for the unable,
It's weak we hate and we look down on the neighbor the doppelganger
With the answers, hope in itself is good but hopeless dealers of
Soul-selling are the kingpins of side street, elevators and reflections

⭐

WHY DON'T YOU LOOK?

There is an orange bloom
In winter.

It is like the heart
Of a baby –
Instinct
Pure
Instinct.

TIME FOR GRANTED

There was no time
For please & thank you.
It had to be done
So you'd shut the fuck up.

There was no time
For different size forks.
You had a meal
You had a meal.

And definitely no time
For non
Sense as
Time = blood.

PIECES

In the valley
Where the dogs
Don't let you
Sleep we'll sleep
Tonight.

In your house

When they don't
Understand me
And I'm itching
You know.

By the stream
Dry and
Deserted you
Hold my hand,
There's still some
Left.

We go to church,
Me and you,
Us and them,
Men and women,
We listen and
Bow, God's
Listening, to
Learn He
Must
Listen to me,
How sad I am
And nobody's
Listening, and later
The rain's battering
Our half-broken
Umbrella,

Jesus loves you, my girl,
But I adore you
Scented off the land
Moaning that the poetry's
Making me sad, hacking
Me to pieces.

⭐

LACU SĂRAT

In the salty lake
You can resuscitate
The flat, deaf,
Divided

By the time you
Leave, by the time
You feel, by the
Time you think

What you see is
Sky and what you
Have is gold –
Been telling you

Relax, breathe, stop
Look the watch
Sank, it's gone

So wait as

Stars work,

His feet itch, an

Ant

Drowns

⭐

FAMILY

Yeah family

That's what I remember

Him ranting about.

Family

Fucking family.

Family

Where you serve and get served

Note

Where YOU are served,

Only YOU.

I remember him

Ranting about

Family

As if family

Drove him,

As if family

Was the center

Of everything

And if you fuck up

There's always the

Family

To hold you while you

Cry,

And if you give up

There's always the

Family

To remind you

That

You can't afford to

Give up,

That you must carry on

For their sake.

You with the family monkey on your back.

And love,

Well love

Is a

Pinch of salt

On your tender

Dish,

Something that doesn't really

Exist,

A little myth

The rich bastards made up

To make the poor darlings

Believe in something better.

Here's my family…

Wolf cubs,

Lonely,

Cold,

Crazy,

In the clear

The bear

Comes –

Dinnertime.

★

SAD SONG

Terrible

Beautiful

Solemn

Faith…

When will you leave me?

When I'm weakest?

When I'm helpless?

Your crying mouth

With your talking eyes

All the apples we had

They surrender

Bleeding hearts

When will you tell me?
When I'm weakest?
When I'm helpless?

⭐

ANSWERS

I'm waiting for an answer from you.
I've been waiting for a day
Disappointed that it hasn't come.
Will it come? Is the answer worth the question?
I'm thinking about my grandfather
And my mother
And how this relates to it all.
The bird bounced off the window
As I filled up
The beer will answer for me.
You're all a bunch of scum,
I said,
You're all lost in the dirt.

⭐

REAL PEOPLE

Are sleeping on benches
And sharing their food

With strays.
They don't give a fuck
About economics.

They're much more
Much more much
More much more
Pathetic
Than you could ever be.

⭐

ALL MY LIFE

Been sticking my neck out
For truth,
Only to be lying
All day long.
Been shaking my head
And disagreeing,
Been asking questions
Only to have starved the self
Of substance.
Been fighting against
The non-existent,
The neutral, passivity,
The submissive which
Has found me
Boneless, heartless

And dismissive.
Oh the passion beyond fashion,
Looking out towards you
With a thrashing headache.

THE FIRE

A warm day, in the shade,
There's no putting off
Look straight into the fire, calm fear,
Right and left
Where the flames cripple your veins.
It's ok, heat will do that,
It's the weather, the atmosphere,
The ghost behind the bookcase.
Meanwhile, listen to the rabid words of faith
And stare into the Mona Lisa eyes of Jesus.
Don't forget the fire.

SELF PORTRAIT

I am nothing
But a slab of meat
Dumped on a chair.
I am everything
As a slab of meat

Weighing down the chair.
I am a thin slab of meat
And an implosion of blood
And a character study of loss
And a modern ageist
And a dot with a name
And a forgotten hurricane
And a re-branded dinosaur
Planning an escape.

⭐

QUIET

Tata became very quiet. Almost always looked upset.
I regret not having asked him why but, at the time,
I was afraid. Maybe he would smack me for asking…

I should've asked "What's wrong tata?
"What's made you feel like this?"
Mind you, it was probably the everyday.

Now nobody asks me why I'm so quiet, so upset looking,
And I gather nobody really cares why,
But maybe somebody does.

Maybe somebody wants to ask
"What's wrong Bogdan?
"What's made you feel like this?"

MATADOR

Yester night could not sleep
Thinking that one-day I would die,
Thinking that tomorrow I would work
And there's no one next to me.
There was a cold space beside me.

Yester night I heard a noise from beyond,
Perhaps a neighbor or a lion escaped from the zoo
Or maybe a psychopath at my door
Looking to settle an old argument,
Maybe a family member, maybe someone I hurt…

Yester night could not sleep
And itched for waking up and wandering round
But there was no reason to
And I could not think of anything to do
But try again, and again and lose.

And while writing this poem
I realized there was still nobody next to me
And that a poem should be written in loneliness
And suffering and done wholeheartedly
Like a matador, the bull and Hemingway.

HER POEM

The weather was good, a sunny weekend,
We walked briefly through the avenue and saw a crawling
Squirrel carrying broken back feet and staring in pain.
Later we sat and thought about us.
Take the man who bullies my
Place without asking, he's boss and he refuses to see me,
I'm not even a salty mug of tears.
Take the man who keeps handing me nothing guess what I do
I keep on praying to him. He hands me a bare plate,
"Bite this," he says.
And let me tell you about them, these do-gooders and sharpshooters,
Signing here and talking there, deciding who gets the
Swimming pool, who wins the spike, who spins the cash,
Who's left to impale, I'll tell you about these fellows
If you need to know what's going on there ain't much
Going on;
And down the street where I'm not walking,
Or in windy shops, inside brick walls typing up
Lists, where we're hanging on to a penny tree,
In lonely churches nobody's praying and everybody's
Sleeping, here, I'm with you, darling,
Every day I'm with you,
Every night I'm sleeping next to you, and
I know it's unforgivable, my excuse
Is I echo the environment, what's left of my love is

Yours, angel.
There was no one else then in scarce solitude with spare sounds
We touched lips and tried to kiss. I was sick with
Something called ambition, oh well what can we do,
Nothing much I'm told or practically plan what
Ends up being made up.
You want a poem, I'll write you one, I'll write you
Anything beautiful you want.
This poem's yours and nobody else need know.
We're staring at each other like we haven't seen each other
Before, you're the only one I want to see.
Let my eyes fixate on you
Please, don't tell me what to do breaking the spell
Kicking the heart punching the soul, I'll hold you,
We'll lay some of that favorite music on, move awhile,
Sing meanwhile, let me fixate
My eyes on you.
That's right I'm dressed up for judgment day and
Don't go to work today, stay with me in this room.
This poem's yours and the sun can shutdown, the leader
Can kill his followers, civilization can lose, rightfully, but
This poem's yours
With a bird of light attached from my lips
To yours.

⭐
A DELICATE ONE

Tell me, honestly, especially,
If I hold your warm frame
When you sleep
Will you dream of my faith?

Then when I turn round
Mountains separate,
But if I see your face later,
Between eyelashes,
Will you murmur to me
Breathless down water fountain?

⭐
NOW US

Even a dull day
Can have pressed on
Florid rainbows,
For example,
If you strain me
I will peel back my
Timid camera for
We must develop
Seeds, don't
Leave them yawning

There.

Here's in hope

To never forget

Youth, beauty and

Immortality.

⭐

I WOULD LIKE TO

Cry for you tonight

In my room,

By myself,

With the thinking lights

The thought bangers,

Tight-lipped

Losers

Animals.

And I would like to

Cry for you right now.

I know

Nothing else.

⭐

SO PLEASING

Did my poem not please thee?

Did it not fulfill your needs?

Have you dismissed me already?

Before I've started

Cutting bone,

Turning rain into wine,

Words into nymphets…

⭐

BURIED

I believe there was sunshine today

Through the window of the room

And through the shutters of the window

That no one dares look at.

There was a good temperature,

One that does not require much

Or so it felt in the timed minutes

Rushing like mad bulls.

Hemingway's been dead for fifty years.

Later we marched in to home.

Who am I? Who are you?

What's with the flowers?

Who's getting buried?

GOD MATTERS

In a driver's window

In a taxi driver's window

In a long distance driver's window,

In my right pocket.

For the rain has come

And the goats are frying

For the stones fall

But

God matters

To the fingers and the palm

When in the woods

Sticking twigs in eyeballs.

A SONG ABOUT SURVIVAL

Never give in

Never give up

Never give them

Satisfaction

Never let the motherfuckers win

Never never never

Never let the motherfuckers win

Never turn in

Never sing their tune

Never get too fucked up

Too messed up too fed up

Never let go of the priceless

(Your vision)

Never let the motherfuckers win

Never never never

Never let the motherfuckers win

Never cry openly

Never waver

Never let loss

Rejection and death

Point the way,

Never underestimate the

Power of soul

Never but listen,

Play the games and

Treat others ten percent

Better or worse

Than they treat you

And

In the end

Never let these motherfuckers win

Never never never

Never let these motherfuckers win

WHAT AM I DOING HERE?

I told you
The other day
I don't relate to anybody…
Well I've not felt
A part, a whole, an inch
Of belonging.
Maybe a few drinks or
Some laughter…
There is a severe limit.
To and for them
And
To and for me.
I am me, in some way,
Due to them, they,
Sure as a circle, surely,
Exist there and then
And perhaps now.
Tomorrow, I will probably feel
Detached, unattached,
As tomorrow, if
I'm alive, will have
Elements of today.
I will be you but
You will stay you…
Aching through what you have.

Tell me, if I pray plenty
Will I be God's?
Can I be yours
If I am here
And you, like an animal,
Feel my reluctance?
You say asking and complaining
Won't help,
But writing a few words
Might just be an answer
Within an answer.

ROMANIAN DEMOCRACY

That's my father there
Eating his shit in the corner
And my mother
Picking beetles off the wall
And sucking on the legs,
My sister plays with the rats
And my brother?
Well,
My brother has his guts
Stuck through iron girders.

GIVE FOOD

Don't call me romantic,
It's not true
Anymore.

Don't call me melancholy,
It was only
Life.

Don't call my number,
It's off
Especially for you.

Don't look for me,
You'll only find me
Easily.

Not romantic but loving,
Ready to apologies
First.

Quite happy with not much,
Things come things go
As we know.

Line up the photos,

I've seen the smiles of
Jesus and Buddha.
What do you do?
What am I doing?
What are we doing?
Lay out the meal,
Our food dear God
Is all,
Give food dear Lord
To all.

⭐

RUTHLESS

If I try to imagine her alone
Crying to live to see to hear us
For just one more day,
If I begin I must stop there.

You cannot imagine
What it's like to live
With so many ruthless
Lessons that have no meaning,
That are just ruthless.

LOST

Everything is there

To be lost,

Every memory

Correct as it seems,

All our loves,

My dear landscape

Everything is to be

Forgotten and buried

Under deep sleep,

Every godforsaken

Truth, the sun fading

To black.

All the songs

All the views

All the feelings

All the regrets

All the ambitions

All the visions

All the steps

We took, one

By one

Everything but absolutely

Everything is there to be

Lost and forgotten and

Raped by the leftovers,

What was beautiful and

What was ours

Will be lost,

And, my dear,

No tear

No gunshot

Can change

What was ours

And what was

Lost.